A2 Law
UNIT 2571

OCR

Module 2571: Criminal Law 1

Chris Turner & Leon Riley

Philip Allan Updates
Market Place
Deddington
Oxfordshire
OX15 0SE

tel: 01869 338652
fax: 01869 337590
e-mail: sales@philipallan.co.uk
www.philipallan.co.uk

ISBN-13: 978-1-84489-019-4
ISBN-10: 1-84489-019-8

This guide has been written specifically to support students preparing for the OCR A2 Law Unit 2571 examination. The content has been neither approved nor endorsed by OCR and remains the sole responsibility of the authors.

Printed by MPG Books, Bodmin

Environmental information
The paper on which this title is printed is sourced from managed, sustainable forests.

Contents

Introduction

■ ■ ■

Content Guidance

■ ■ ■

Questions and Answers

Introduction

About this guide

This study guide is written for students following the OCR A2 Law course and covers the specification content of **Module 2571: Criminal Law 1**. The selection of the topics in this module is designed to give students a sound introduction to the essential elements for proving criminal liability, both for crimes requiring proof of criminal intent and for crimes of strict liability, where criminal intent is not necessary. The unit examines preliminary, or incomplete, crimes the major one being attempt. The unit also covers the main substantive homicide offences, including murder, the special and partial defences to murder often referred to as voluntary manslaughter, and the different types of involuntary manslaughter where the specific intent required for murder cannot be proved despite the unlawful killing.

There are three sections to this guide:

- **Introduction** — this section gives advice on how to use the guide, some learning strategies, some hints on planning revision, a reminder of the assessment criteria and how to achieve them, and also an explanation of what the exam paper is about and the skills needed to complete it successfully.
- **Content guidance** — this section sets out the specification content for Unit 2571, and the key knowledge for successful completion of the exam. It is broken down into subsections in the same way as the specification and provides a structure for your learning. Where cases or statutes are referred to, you will need to study these in more detail for a fuller understanding.
- **Questions and answers** — this section provides sample answers to typical examination questions on each topic area. Each question is followed by an A-, a C- and an E-grade answer. Examiner comments show how marks are awarded or why they are withheld.

How to use this guide

The Content Guidance section covers all the elements of the Unit 2571 specification, breaking down each topic into manageable sections for initial study and later revision. It is not intended to be a comprehensive and detailed set of notes for the unit — the material needs to be supplemented by further reading from textbooks and by your own class notes.

At the end of each topic section, you may find it useful to compile a summary of the factual material under appropriate headings. Ideally, you should incorporate additional material drawn from a number of sources: classroom teaching, textbooks, quality newspapers, law journals and legal websites. When you have finished compiling your notes, you can tackle the questions in the third section of the guide. Read the questions carefully and answer them fully. You should then read the sample A-grade answers and compare these with your own answers to identify where you could have gained more marks in order to achieve a higher grade. Compare your answers with the C- and E-grade answers in order to get an indication of how well you are performing. The examiner comments will help you to understand what factors can limit your marks and how you can attain the higher grades.

Learning strategies

A2 is very different from AS and more is required of you in the examinations. While the good knowledge and understanding you may have of the various topics studied during your course is still important at A2, you will need a greater depth of under-standing and will need to learn many more cases. For this reason, you must keep a clear and accurate set of notes. Another significant difference at A2 is that you are expected to have better-developed critical ability, meaning that you will need to show that you can discuss the law at length in the essay questions for Section A and apply the law effectively to factual situations in the problem question for Section B.

You should employ an effective learning strategy as follows:

- Try to take notes in class in a logical and methodical way — don't just write down everything that the teacher says.
- Make sure that you read your notes again after each class — don't leave it too long or the information will not be fresh in your mind.
- If you don't understand something in your notes, read about it in your textbook or ask your teacher. Make sure you correct your notes so that you can understand them.
- Do all the reading that your teacher suggests and also try to read around the subject to build up greater knowledge and understanding. If you have spaces in your class notes, you can add additional information from your reading. If not, you should rewrite your notes to incorporate it.
- Build up a good understanding of the principles of law that come from the individual cases and try to remember the case names by testing yourself frequently.
- Use a legal dictionary so that you become familiar with all the appropriate legal terminology.

Revision planning

Revision is not the same as learning. All of the learning strategies mentioned above should have been covered during the course and you should have a complete and accurate set of notes when you begin your revision. If you have to learn the material from scratch before the exam, then you are putting extra pressure on yourself.

There are various rules for good revision practice that you should follow:

- Organise your material before you begin. You will be revising more than one subject, which will have many topics. It will help your revision process if you have separate folders for each subject. Use folder dividers for individual topics, so that you can turn straight to the topic you wish to revise.

- Organise your time effectively. Thirty minutes preparing a revision timetable will save you a lot of time later on. Divide the time you have available by the topic areas. Identify how many times you can revise them and create a chart.
- Use effective revision aids to help compress the subject matter or put it into visual form to make the process simpler and less time consuming. Examples are key facts charts, mind maps, flowcharts and diagrams.
- Make revision cards on all the leading cases.
- Ask your friends and family to test you on important knowledge.
- Practise past papers. The more familiar you are with the style of questions that you can expect, the more confident you will become in answering them in the exam. Tackling problem questions in particular will help to build your understanding, since the law makes more sense when it is applied to factual situations.
- Do your revision in short bursts. The longer you sit looking at your notes in one session, the more likely you are to get bored and not take anything in. Take plenty of breaks between sessions.

Assessment objectives

Assessment objectives (AOs) are the measures against which examiners test your knowledge, understanding and legal skills. They are common to AS and A2 units and are intended to assess a candidate's ability to:

- AO1 — recall, select and develop knowledge and understanding of legal princi-ples accurately by means of example and citation, i.e. your ability to remember the appropriate law, including cases or statute where appropriate.
- AO2 — analyse legal material, issues and situations, and evaluate and apply the appropriate legal rules and principles, i.e. your ability to engage in a balanced discussion, offering points of criticism in essays, and to apply legal rules to factual situations in problem-style questions.
- AO3 — present a logical and coherent argument, communicating relevant material in a clear and effective manner, using appropriate legal terminology, i.e. your ability to give legal information and to discuss or apply it clearly, as well as to spell, punctuate and use grammar accurately.

Remember that in OCR A2 exams there are five levels of assessment, while in AS exams there are only four. This means that you have to show more knowledge and better analysis or application skills in order to reach the highest mark level.

For AO1, this means that as well as demonstrating that you have well-developed knowledge, as you did for AS, it must be wide ranging.

For AO2 you must show a high level of analysis or application, and not just analyse the more obvious points or apply the obvious law, as would have been expected of you at AS.

When you sit AS examinations, you have only completed 1 year of the A-level course. After 2 years, you are expected to have gained more knowledge and to have developed better skills. Don't think that, just because you got a good grade at AS, you will automatically do so at A2.

There is also an extra level for AO3, so your communication skills should have improved, and for the highest level you will be expected to write with few, if any, errors of spelling, punctuation or grammar.

The examination

Unit 2571 is made up of two sections and in 90 minutes you have to answer one question from a choice of two in each section. All questions are worth 50 marks, made up of 25 marks for AO1, 20 marks for AO2 and 5 marks for AO3.

Section A contains essay-style questions, where you are expected to show your knowledge of the topic areas and also to analyse and/or evaluate. You must be able to identify the critical purpose of the question asked, to engage in a balanced discussion looking at both sides of an argument, and finally to reach conclusions resulting from that discussion.

Section B questions involve legal problem solving. You will be provided with a factual scenario and you will then have to identify the areas of law that could be used to resolve the issues that arise from the scenario. In criminal law, this means that you will need to identify offences that may arise from the facts, as well as possible defences. In Criminal Law 1, problems are less likely to involve multiple issues because there are only a few substantive offences in the specification content. You are likely to see problems on murder, with causation as a major issue. Issues concerning attempt could also be included. Questions on diminished responsibility and provocation are common too, and do not forget that there are often different possibilities arising from the same set of facts. Involuntary manslaughter is often examined as a problem-solving question.

Planning is an important part of achieving high marks in any examination. In the case of essays for Section A, remember the importance of structuring your answer. Your answer should include:

- an introduction identifying what the question is asking
- a balanced discussion using cases, sections of Acts and legal principles in support of your answer
- a reasoned conclusion deriving from your discussion

Structure is also important in the problem-solving questions for Section B. You must:

- identify, for each individual aspect of the problem, the key facts on which resolution of the problem is based
- define the appropriate law
- apply the law to the facts
- reach sound conclusions based on your application of the law

Remember also to:
- read the question thoroughly, so that you are certain what it is asking for
- plan your answer briefly at the start of the exam to ensure you only use relevant information
- always use law (cases or statutes) in support of your arguments for essays or in your application for problem questions
- avoid excessive use of the facts of cases — it is the principle that is important
- make sure that you answer the question set

Content
Guidance

The material covered in Unit 2571: Criminal Law 1, is divided into three sections. The first is concerned with the essential elements of crimes and is vital to the understanding of all substantive offences, whether in Criminal Law 1 or Criminal Law 2. In this section of the Criminal Law specification content, it is absolutely vital for you to gain a good understanding of some fairly difficult concepts. The second section covers some preliminary crimes, often referred to as inchoate or incomplete crimes. The third section covers the major crimes of homicide including murder, partial defences to murder contained in the Homicide Act 1957 (an area often referred to as voluntary manslaughter), and involuntary manslaughter (killing that lacks the necessary criminal intent for murder). This final section reinforces the first, as it includes many of the cases that you will have learned when covering the essential elements of crimes. The areas covered in Unit 2571 are:

Principles of criminal liability

Actus reus
- Voluntary and involuntary conduct
- Omissions as *actus reus*
- *Actus reus* and causation

Mens rea
- Intention
- Recklessness
- Gross negligence
- Specific intent and basic intent
- Transferred malice
- The coincidence of the *actus reus* and the *mens rea*

Strict liability
- Factors significant in establishing strict liability
- Arguments in favour of strict liability
- Arguments against strict liability
- Suggested reform

Secondary participation
- Principals and accessories
- The nature of secondary participation
- The *actus reus* in secondary participation
- The *mens rea* in secondary participation

Preliminary crimes

Incitement
- Incitement and the *actus reus*
- Incitement and the *mens rea*

Conspiracy
- Statute conspiracy
- Common-law conspiracy
- Conspiracy with a foreign element

Attempts
- Attempts and the *actus reus*
- Attempts and the *mens rea*

Fatal offences against the person

Murder
- The *actus reus* of murder
- The *mens rea* of murder

Voluntary manslaughter
- Diminished responsibility
- Provocation
- Failed suicide pacts

Involuntary manslaughter
- Constructive manslaughter (unlawful act manslaughter)
- Gross negligence manslaughter
- Reckless manslaughter
- Reform of involuntary manslaughter

Principles of criminal liability

Actus reus

All crimes, with the exception of those identified as 'strict liability', require proof of both a criminal act and a criminal intention. This requirement comes from the maxim *'actus non facit reum, nisi mens sit rea'*, meaning that an act by itself will not make a person guilty unless the mind is guilty.

The *actus reus* is the factual part of the crime and is often referred to by criminal lawyers as the 'external element' of the crime. The criminal act can involve different categories of fact (some crimes involve all of these but sometimes one alone is enough):

- **Conduct.** This refers to the active part of the *actus reus*, i.e. what the defendant does. Sometimes the *actus reus* can *only* be based on conduct, e.g. perjury. There does not always have to be a positive act, and in some circumstances, a failure to act or an omission can lead to criminal liability. In rarer circumstances, a mere 'state of affairs' can be sufficient.
- **Circumstances.** This refers to the context in which the act becomes a crime. Sometimes an act may be legitimate and not criminal at all if the circumstances are different, e.g. consent to an assault that occurs in a sporting context, where the laws of the game have been followed.
- **Consequences.** Some crimes are called 'result' crimes because whatever the act, the crime is incomplete until a specific result occurs, e.g. homicide offences such as murder and manslaughter require a death.

Voluntary and involuntary conduct

The *actus reus* of a crime only exists where the defendant's conduct is voluntary. As a result, if the defendant's act or omission is beyond his or her control, then there is no criminal liability (*Kay* v *Butterworth*, 1945). Since voluntary conduct must also be conscious conduct, if the defendant is unconscious or unaware, then *actus reus* is missing. In this case the defence of non-insane automatism may apply. However, this automatism is difficult to demonstrate satisfactorily, as illustrated by *Broome* v *Perkins* (1987).

The Law Commission in the Draft Criminal Code suggested an alternative definition whereby a person is not guilty of an offence if:

- he or she acts in a state of automatism, i.e. the act is a reflex, spasm or convulsion, or it occurs while the person is in a condition of sleep, unconsciousness, impaired consciousness or otherwise, depriving him/her of effective control of the act
- the act or condition is the result neither of anything done or omitted with the fault required for the offence, nor of voluntary intoxication

Sometimes, however, a defendant can be convicted even in the absence of voluntary conduct because he or she falls within a 'state of affairs' that is prohibited by the criminal law (*R* v *Larsonneur*, 1933). This seems unfair because the defendant has no control over the state of affairs and there appears to be an absence of *actus reus*. However, the principle has been approved more than once (*Winzar* v *Chief Constable of Kent*, 1983).

Omissions as *actus reus*

On the whole, English law requires a positive act. There is no provision for a 'Good Samaritan' law, so it is generally not possible to impose liability for a failure to act. However, because of the presence of duty situations in English law, it is possible to be criminally liable for a failure to act in certain defined circumstances, where this failure amounts to a breach of a specific duty to act.

The situations are limited but the *actus reus* can include an omission where a duty to act arises:
- under a contract, e.g. *R* v *Pittwood* (1902)
- from specific relationships such as parent and child, e.g. *R* v *Gibbons and Proctor* (1918), or doctor and patient, e.g. *Airedale NHS Trust* v *Bland* (1993)
- from a voluntary assumption of care for another, e.g. *R* v *Stone and Dobinson* (1977)
- from a statutory duty to act, e.g. *R* v *Dytham* (1979)
- as a result of the defendant's prior dangerous conduct, e.g. *R* v *Miller* (1983)

Actus reus and causation

Since the *actus reus* is based on the defendant's voluntary conduct, causation can be an issue in determining criminal liability in 'result' crimes such as murder or manslaughter, when the identity of the party responsible for the actual outcome is called into question.

Causation is measured in two ways:
- **Factual causation.** The question of the defendant's criminal liability is determined on the basis of the 'but for' test, i.e. but for the defendant's criminal act or omission would the victim have suffered the damage? If the answer is no, then the defendant is criminally liable. If something else is the cause of the damage, then the defendant is not liable (*R* v *White*, 1910).
- **Legal causation.** This is a more complex issue and concerns whether or not the defendant can be said to be legally responsible for the result. For instance, in *R* v *Pagett* (1983), the victim was killed by police gunshots during a siege. However, the defendant had used the victim as a human shield during a gunfire exchange with police officers in a dark alleyway and so was legally the cause of the victim's death.

A number of factors need to be considered in determining causation:
- whether the defendant's act is a sufficiently substantial cause (*R* v *Adams*, 1957)

- the effect of cumulative causes — compare *R* v *Benge* (1865) with *R* v *Armstrong* (1989)
- the effect of intervening events — generally, if a *novus actus interveniens* (a new intervening act) breaks the chain of causation, it relieves the defendant of liability because the intervening act is then the real cause; however, merely switching off the life-support machine of a victim declared brainstem dead does not break the chain of causation (*R* v *Malcharek*, 1981)
- the defendant must 'take his victim how he finds him', so that the defendant is not excused where, for example, a Jehovah's Witness has refused a subsequent blood transfusion (*R* v *Blaue*, 1975)
- the fact that subsequent negligent medical treatment only breaks the chain of causation if it is the actual operative cause of death, and the defendant's act or omission can no longer be seen to be connected to the result (*R* v *Jordan*, 1956); the preferred position is that which occurred in *R* v *Smith* (1959) and *R* v *Cheshire* (1991)

Mens rea

In criminal law (with the exception of strict liability offences), a defendant can be guilty of an offence only if he or she can be shown to have acted with criminal intent. This criminal intent is referred to as *mens rea*.

Mens rea is potentially complex as there are different levels and the required *mens rea* varies from crime to crime.

Sometimes certain aspects of the *mens rea* are not only a state of mind but also descriptive of other aspects of the *mens rea*, e.g. a deception by deliberate or reckless intent, or there may be an ulterior intent, e.g. a reckless wounding with the intent of committing grievous bodily harm.

The external elements of the crime (the *actus reus*) and the conduct of the accused (the *mens rea*) constitute the separate ingredients of a crime. In each criminal case, the prosecution is obliged to prove at least the minimum level of criminal intent appropriate to the individual crime.

There are three types of criminal intent (depending on the individual crime):
- intention
- recklessness
- gross negligence

Intention

Intention, sometimes referred to as 'full-blown intention', is the highest level of *mens rea*. In *R* v *Mohan* (1976), the court suggested that this form of intention occurs when the defendant decides to bring about a prohibited consequence, irrespective of whether he or she also *desires* to bring about that consequence. The Law Commission in the Draft Criminal Code has suggested that the definition should be: 'a person acts intentionally with respect to a result when he or she acts either in order to bring it about or being aware that it will occur in the ordinary course of events.'

There are two types of intention:
- direct intent
- oblique intent

Direct intent

Direct intent is straightforward. It occurs when the result is actually desired by the defendant. In this sense, it is immaterial that the desired result is achieved, since an inchoate offence is still possible, e.g. attempted murder. Motive is also irrelevant, since this is not the same as intent (*Yip Chiu-cheung* v *R*, 1994).

Oblique intent

Oblique intent (also known as 'foresight intent') is where intent has to be inferred from the evidence. This covers the situation where the consequence is foreseen by the defendant as virtually certain, although it is not desired for its own sake, and the defendant goes ahead with his/her actions anyway. Inevitably, this type of intent is measured against foresight of those consequences, i.e. how likely the result was to occur. For this reason, it has caused many problems. Many of the cases that deal with how oblique intent can be measured are murder cases, and the House of Lords has reached many confusing and often conflicting interpretations.

At one time, foresight was measured objectively according to the standards of the reasonable person and classed as equivalent to intent (*DPP* v *Smith*, 1961). However, this was unsatisfactory because it negated any need to show the defendant's mental state and so it was remedied by s.8 of the **Criminal Law Act 1967**. This states that a jury, in determining whether a person has committed an offence:

- *shall not* be bound in law to infer that he intended or foresaw a result of his actions by reason only of its being a natural and probable consequence of those actions but
- *shall* decide whether he did intend or foresee that result by reference to all the evidence, drawing such inferences from the evidence as appear proper in the circumstances

Foresight was then linked to probability in *Hyam* v *DPP* (1975), but on a split decision 3:2 with each judge giving different reasons for the result, thus confusing the issue still further. This approach was rejected as being too broad and ambiguous in *R* v *Moloney* (1985). Lord Bridge's direction was that intent could only be inferred where death or serious injury was a 'natural consequence' of the defendant's act and the defendant foresaw that this was the case.

However, this narrowed the test too far and was still ambiguous, so Lord Scarman developed guidelines for judges and juries in *R* v *Hancock and Shankland* (1986), suggesting that foresight was not a legal test but only factual evidence from which to infer intent. He stated that the greater the probability of a consequence, the greater the likelihood that it was foreseen, and that the more likely it was foreseen the more likely it was intended. This test was redefined into a model direction by Lord Lane in *R v Nedrick* (1986). The court made the following points:

- If a consequence is desired, then as a matter of law it is intended.
- Where foresight of consequences is absent, then as a matter of law there is no intent.
- The degree of foresight in between these points is a question of fact for the jury to decide, with guidance from the judge, in order to determine existence or otherwise of intention. (Foresight is not the same as intention but only evidence from which intent can be inferred.)
- In those cases where intent needs to be inferred, the jury should ask two questions:
    — How probable was the consequence which resulted from the defendant's act?
    — Did the defendant foresee those consequences?
    The jury should only then infer intention if death or serious injury was a virtual certainty and the defendant appreciated that this was the case.

This 'model direction' was initially rejected by the Court of Appeal in *R v Woollin* (1997), but the Court was overruled by the House of Lords. While the Court of Appeal disapproved of the use of the two questions from *Nedrick*, the model direction was approved with the word 'find' being used in place of the word 'infer'. Subsequently, the Court of Appeal in *R v Matthews and Alleyne* (2003) has confirmed that foresight of consequences is only evidence of intention, and it is not automatically intention.

Recklessness

Recklessness is a lesser mental state than actual intention, so it is not the same as desiring the consequences, as would be the case with direct intent. It is arguable, however, whether recklessness is merely a step away from oblique intent, and the distinction may not be so easy to define.

The defining feature of recklessness is the taking of an unjustified risk, i.e. the defendant appreciated the existence of the risk but nevertheless carried on and took it. In determining whether the defendant was reckless, the jury would need to decide:

- how likely the risked consequence was
- the social utility of the acts which created the risk
- the practicability of any possible precautions that could have been taken to avoid the risk

Recklessness has traditionally been measured in two different ways:

- objective recklessness
- subjective recklessness

Objective recklessness

Objective recklessness stems from the case of *R v Caldwell* (1981). It works on the basis of asking whether a reasonable person in the defendant's circumstances would have appreciated that the risk existed. If so, the defendant could be guilty on the basis of recklessness, regardless of whether he or she actually did recognise the risk.

This objective standard of recklessness, however, had the obvious potential to cause injustice, such as in the classic example of *Elliott* v *C* (1983). *Caldwell* concerned criminal damage, but objective recklessness caused even greater controversy when applied in other areas, e.g. causing death by reckless driving (*R* v *Lawrence*, 1982). Therefore, it was later held that it could only be applied in cases of criminal damage. Now, following *R* v *G and another* (2003), the House of Lords has overruled *Caldwell* and only subjective recklessness can be used.

Subjective recklessness

Subjective recklessness derives from *R* v *Cunningham* (1957) and is based on asking whether or not the defendant realised the existence of a risk but nevertheless went on to take it. If so, then the defendant is guilty.

Subjective recklessness is now the only type of recklessness accepted by the courts. It had, in any case, already been accepted in all offences where the definition of the offence included the word 'maliciously' (*R* v *Savage*, 1992).

One problem has been identified in relation to subjective recklessness: the so-called lacuna, or loophole. Here, the defendant might claim that he or she honestly did not believe that there was a risk, or that he or she had eliminated the risk, in which case, if this is accepted, there can be no conviction. However, successful cases demonstrating a lacuna are rare (*R* v *Merrick*, 1996), as the point on which the defendant is mistaken must exclude any possibility of risk (*R* v *Reid*, 1992).

The Draft Criminal Code favours use of subjective recklessness only.

Gross negligence

Gross negligence applies only in the context of manslaughter. Negligence is a civil concept, where objective standards are common and are measured against the reasonable person, and where the standard of proof is lower than for criminal law. Consequently, there is some conceptual overlap with *Caldwell* recklessness and some of the same difficulties arise.

Gross negligence can include:
- contemplating a risk and wrongly concluding that it does not exist
- recognising a risk and taking inadequate steps to avoid it

Gross negligence is now the proper test in manslaughter (*R* v *Adomako*, 1995):
- Liability first depends on the existence of a duty owed by the defendant to the victim.
- The test is whether the defendant's behaviour is so negligent in all the circumstances as to justify a conviction for manslaughter.
- This test is one purely for the jury to decide.

One potential benefit of gross negligence is that it may make it easier to bring a charge of corporate manslaughter.

Specific intent and basic intent

It is also possible to classify intent in criminal offences as either:

- basic intent, where the *mens rea* does not extend past the *actus reus*, e.g. rape
- specific intent, where the *mens rea* does extend past the *actus reus*, e.g. murder (where the unlawful killing must be carried out with malice aforethought), or theft (where the appropriation of the property belonging to another person must be done dishonestly and with the intention permanently to deprive another of that property)

In the case of crimes of basic intent, the necessary *mens rea* can be either intention or recklessness. However, with crimes of specific intent, the *mens rea* requires either direct intent or oblique intent, or that one element of the *mens rea* goes beyond the *actus reus* (e.g. the intention permanently to deprive in theft).

Another possible distinction between basic intent and specific intent is that intoxication may provide a defence for crimes of specific intent, but it can never provide a defence for crimes of basic intent, because there is recklessness in becoming intoxicated.

Transferred malice

A defendant may be liable for a criminal offence, even though the victim is different to the one intended, or the consequence occurs in a different way (*R* v *Latimer*, 1886), in which case the *mens rea* transfers to the other victim.

However, the *mens rea* cannot be transferred to a substantially different offence (*R* v *Pembliton*, 1874).

The coincidence of the *actus reus* and the *mens rea*

Generally, both the act and the mental state must be contemporaneous for an offence to be committed. However, the courts have been quite liberal in their interpretation of the coincidence of the two, obviously for pragmatic reasons and also to ensure that justice prevails over technicality.

In this way, the courts have accepted that there is still coincidence of the *actus reus* and the *mens rea* in the case of:

- continuing acts (*Fagan* v *Metropolitan Police Commissioner*, 1969). These are generally those cases where the *mens rea* is not formed until after the conduct of the *actus reus* has begun and the link is that it continues (*R* v *Kaitamaki*, 1984).
- cases amounting to single transactions (*R* v *Thabo Meli*, 1954). These are generally where the *actus reus* is not complete at the time there is *mens rea* (*R* v *Church*, 1966 and *R* v *Le Brun*, 1991).

Strict liability

Strict liability simply means that there is no requirement to prove a mental element in respect of one or more areas of the *actus reus*. However, the concept is not that straightforward and it is often easier to show *how* the principle of strict liability operates than *when* it operates. It is generally an unclear and imprecise area.

Strict liability can be complicated because one or more of the general defences may be available. Certainly in the case of strict liability offences deriving from statute, the statute itself may indicate available defences. An obvious example is the due diligence defence that is common in offences involving consumer protection.

On this basis, strict liability should not be confused with absolute liability, where even a lack of voluntary conduct would not prevent liability (*R* v *Larsonneur*, 1933). It is possible, however, that the defendant could be liable merely for his or her blameless inadvertence (e.g. s.4 of the **Road Traffic Act 1988**, driving with excess alcohol in the blood), which applies regardless of the reason for it.

The majority of strict liability crimes are statutory, so the offences are mostly regulatory. However, some strict liability offences can involve imprisonment (*Gammon (Hong Kong) Ltd* v *AG of Hong Kong*, 1984).

There are a few common-law strict liability offences. The three main ones are public nuisance, criminal libel and blasphemous libel (*R* v *Lemon and Gay News*, 1979).

Strict liability becomes a problem when a statute is silent on the issue of *mens rea*. The general presumption is that a crime always requires *mens rea*, unless the contrary is expressly stated by Parliament (*Sweet* v *Parsley*, 1970). However, this is a refutable presumption (*Pharmaceutical Society of Great Britain* v *Storkwain*, 1986) and it is possible to be convicted of a strict liability offence even though the defendant is unaware of the fact of committing the wrong (*Cundy* v *Le Cocq*, 1884). To complicate the area still further, strict liability offences have been identified in the past with an element of *mens rea* (*R* v *Prince*, 1895, although this case was not followed in *B* v *DPP*, 2000).

Factors significant in establishing strict liability

The modern approach of the courts to strict liability was put clearly by Lord Scarman in *Gammon (Hong Kong) Ltd* v *AG of Hong Kong* (1984):

(1) There is a presumption of law that *mens rea* is required before a person can be guilty of a criminal offence.

(2) The presumption is particularly strong where the offence is 'truly criminal' in character.

(3) The presumption applies to statutory offences, and can be displaced only if this is clearly, or by necessary implication, the effect of the statute.

(4) The only situation in which the presumption can be displaced is where the statute is concerned with an issue of social concern.

content guidance

(5) Public safety is such an issue.

(6) Even where the statute is concerned with such an issue, the presumption of *mens rea* stands, unless it can be shown that the creation of strict liability will be effective to promote the objects of the statute by encouraging greater vigilance to prevent the commission of the prohibited act.

It is difficult to say when the courts will identify that an offence is strict liability. However, the following guidelines be used:

The statutory context — the wording of the Act
There is no guarantee as to which words will lead to strict liability, but there are some patterns:

- The words 'permitting', 'allowing', 'knowingly' or 'intentionally' usually imply that there is a requirement of *mens rea* because they clearly indicate an awareness (compare *James and Sons* v *Smee*, 1955 with *Green* v *Burnett*, 1955).
- Where the word 'cause' is used, common sense often dictates that there is no requirement for *mens rea* (*Wrothwell* v *Yorkshire Water Authority*, 1984).
- The word 'possession' usually requires some form of knowledge (*Warner* v *Metropolitan Police Commissioner*, 1969).
- It may be that the absence of a particular word means that strict liability will be accepted (*Kirkland* v *Robinson*, 1987).

The social context — crimes and quasi-crimes
The House of Lords in *Sweet* v *Parsley* (1970) identified that crimes should be distinguished from regulatory offences that are for the convenience of the public. Crimes always need *mens rea*, whereas regulatory offences rarely do. Clearly, the more dangerous the activity involved, then the more likely it is that the courts will apply the presumption of *mens rea* (*R* v *Howells*, 1977). Further, offences may be accepted by the courts as strict liability for pure reasons of public policy (*R* v *Blake*, 1997).

Strict liability offences can often apply to regulate:
- sale of food and drink
- licensing of activities
- protection of the environment
- supply of drugs and pharmaceuticals
- road traffic activities

The severity of the punishment
Usually, the greater the available punishment the more likely it is that *mens rea* is required, but this is not an absolute test (*Gammon (Hong Kong) Ltd* v *AG of Hong Kong*, 1984). Even crimes attaching quite severe punishment have been accepted as strict liability (*R* v *Champ*, 1981).

It may be that a court needs to look at all possible pointers, a fact that reinforces the view of the Law Commission that, when enacting new offences, Parliament should be clear in the Act whether or not the offence is strict liability (*B (a minor)* v *DPP*, 2000).

It is common in modern statutes to include certain defences to strict liability offences. An example of these is the due diligence or third party defence that appears in consumer protection statutes such as the **Trade Descriptions Act 1968** and the **Misuse of Drugs Act 1971**.

Arguments in favour of strict liability

- helps to protect the public
- is easier for the police and for bodies such as Trading Standards to enforce
- can act as a deterrent to bad business practice
- creates recognisable standards
- reduces time and cost of court appearances
- follows the fault principle in tort
- reduces the evidential burden
- is always possible for Parliament to provide a defence where appropriate
- levels of blame can be accounted for by sentencing

Arguments against strict liability

- denies people the chance to state a case
- does not necessarily raise standards
- may punish people who have, in fact, taken proper care
- people may take the blame for another individual's wrongdoing
- can offend human rights principles

Suggested reform

The Law Commission has suggested reforms that are contained in the Draft Criminal Code. It says that 'every offence requires a fault element of recklessness with respect to each of its elements other than fault elements, unless otherwise provided'. The main effect of such a reform would be that no offence would be taken as being strict liability unless Parliament had expressly stated it as being so in the Act.

Secondary participation

Principals and accessories

A principal offender is one who actually causes the *actus reus* of the offence through his or her actions. There can be joint principals, where two or more people carry out the offence and each of them also has the necessary *mens rea*. An 'accessory' or secondary participant, on the other hand, is a person who contributes to the commission of the crime but is not the person actually bringing about the *actus reus*.

It is also possible that the person carrying out the *actus reus* is not the principal offender. This is called 'innocent agency' because the agent was merely being used by the principal offender and usually does not have the necessary *mens rea*, or possibly lacks the capacity to commit the crime, for example because of being a child (*R* v *Michael*, 1840 and *R* v *Cogan and Leak*, 1976).

Some offences may occur where there are two or more principal offenders, but even then there can be secondary participation (*R* v *Jefferson*, 1994). Even if it is not known which is the principal offender and which is the accomplice, both can still be charged (*R* v *Mohan*, 1967). This is because it only needs to be shown that each aided, abetted, counselled or procured the other (*R* v *Russell and Russell*, 1987).

There can be many parties to a crime, each committing different offences. For example, imagine that D decides that he wants to kill W:
- A encourages D to carry out the killing.
- B supplies D with a weapon.
- C tells D where W can be found.
- E then drives D to W's house and acts as a lookout.
- F, who is present in the house, shouts encouragement to D to kill W.

D is the principal offender. All the other parties are accomplices (or secondary participants), but in different ways.

The nature of secondary participation

The rules on secondary participation in the case of indictable offences are contained in s.8 of the **Accessories and Abettors Act 1861**: '...whosoever shall aid, abet, counsel or procure the commission of any indictable offence...shall be liable to be tried as a principal offender.' By s.44 of the **Magistrates Court Act 1980**, the same principle applies to summary offences.

Conviction as an accomplice is possible in one of four different ways according to Lord Widgery LCJ in *Attorney General's References (No. 1 of 1975)*:
- **Aiding.** This is being voluntarily present at the crime and assisting in the crime or in the preparation of the crime (*Tuck* v *Robson*, 1970).
- **Abetting.** This is inciting, encouraging, or instigating the crime, usually at the scene (*Wilcox* v *Jeffery*, 1951 and *Forman* v *Ford*, 1988).
- **Counselling.** This is giving advice and encouragement, but before the crime is carried out (*R* v *Bainbridge*, 1959).
- **Procuring.** This is defined as 'to produce by endeavour' the commission of the crime by the principal (*A-G's Reference (No. 1 of 1975)*, *R* v *Millward*, 1994, *R* v *Bourne*, 1952 and *R* v *Coogan and Leake*, 1976).

Lord Widgery in *A-G's Reference (No. 1 of 1975)* defined the four different ways and identified that the common-law distinction between the four still applies:
- An accomplice who is present at the scene of the substantive offence is either an aider or an abettor.
- An accomplice who is not at the scene is either a counsellor or a procurer.

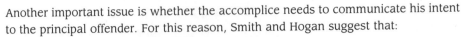

Another important issue is whether the accomplice needs to communicate his intent to the principal offender. For this reason, Smith and Hogan suggest that:

- 'procuring' implies causation but not consensus
- 'abetting' and 'counselling' both imply consensus but not causation
- 'aiding' requires actual assistance but neither consensus nor causation is necessary

In practice, it has been argued that there is no real conceptual difference between the four terms. They all concern conduct by the accessory which helps or encourages the principal in some way to commit the crime.

The Law Commission has recommended that there should be only two offences:

- an inchoate offence of assisting crime
- an inchoate offence of encouraging crime (similar to the present offence of incitement)

The *actus reus* in secondary participation

There are four things to consider about the *actus reus* in secondary participation:

- It requires active conduct. Mere passive behaviour, such as watching the offence take place, is insufficient on its own (*R* v *Clarkson*, 1971).
- As a result, the mere fact that the secondary party is present at the scene of the crime is also insufficient on its own (*R* v *Coney*, 1882).
- The mere fact that a person has a relationship with the principal offender is insufficient on its own, without active involvement of some kind (*R* v *Bland*, 1988).
- No conviction as an accessory is possible without the *actus reus* of the major offence (*Thornton* v *Mitchell*, 1940).

The *mens rea* in secondary participation

The *mens rea* in secondary participation has two elements:

- Knowledge that the crime will be committed (*R* v *Bainbridge*, 1960); however, there is no requirement for the accomplice to know the exact crime (*Maxwell* v *DPP for Northern Ireland*, 1979).
- The intention to assist the principal in some way (*Blakely and Sutton* v *Chief Constable of West Mercia*, 1991); it is also possible for this to be implied vicariously (*NCB* v *Gamble*, 1959).

There are defences available to an accessory that include:

- Acting to assist law enforcement (*R* v *Clarke*, 1985).
- Acting to prevent the harmful consequences of the crime (*Gillick* v *West Norfolk and Wisbech Area Health Authority*, 1986).
- In some circumstances, the accomplice's belief that he or she is legally obliged to act — for example, returning the principal's property which is then used to commit an offence.

Preliminary crimes

Incitement

> **Tip**
>
> Incitement is identified in the specification as 'in outline only', so there is no need for you to have an extensive knowledge of the area. It may only form part of a question.

Incitement is usually a common-law crime and concerns trying to persuade another person to commit an offence. If the offence in question is an indictable offence, the judge has full discretion on sentence. If it is a summary or either-way offence, the sentence is the same.

There are some limited statutory examples of incitement, e.g. incitement to commit murder by s.4 of the **Offences Against the Person Act 1861**, but these are rare.

Smith and Hogan state that 'intention to bring about the criminal result is the essence of incitement'. On the face of it, incitement seems similar to some aspects of secondary participation. It differs because there is no necessity for the crime to be carried out.

Incitement and the *actus reus*

In terms of incitement, the *actus reus* is that the defendant, by means of persuasion, encouragement, threats or pressure, sought to influence another person to commit a crime (*R. R. Board* v *Applin*, 1973).

There is no requirement for the incitement to be directed at a particular individual (*R* v *Most*, 1881 and *Invicta Plastics* v *Clare*, 1976). However, there is no incitement if the act, if performed, would not itself be a crime (*R* v *Whitehouse*, 1977).

Impossibility can be a defence in limited circumstances, where the defendant incites someone to commit a crime using inadequate means, knowing that the crime is impossible whatever means are used (*R* v *Fitzmaurice*, 1983).

Incitement and the *mens rea*

This is simply the intention that the person incited should commit the crime. Therefore, that person need not have *mens rea* for the crime, provided that the inciter believes that he or she would have *mens rea* (*Invicta Plastics* v *Clare*, 1976). As a result, proving *mens rea* should be easy, provided that the inciter knows that a crime would result from the incitement (but see *R* v *Shaw*, 1994).

Conspiracy

Incitement is identified in the specification as 'in outline only', so there is no need for you to have an extensive knowledge of the area. It may only form part of a question.

Conspiracy was traditionally a common-law offence, but was subsequently redefined in statute, while retaining certain areas of the common law. There are now, therefore, two types of conspiracy:

- statutory conspiracy under s.1 of the **Criminal Law Act 1977**
- specific areas of conspiracy remaining under the common law

The definition for statutory conspiracy is provided by s.1 of the **Criminal Law Act 1977**:

> ...if a person agrees with any other person or persons that a course of conduct shall be pursued which...if carried out...either will necessarily amount to...any offence, or would do so but for the existence of facts which render the commission of the offence impossible...

Statute conspiracy

Under the **Criminal Law Act 1977**, the *actus reus* includes:

- an agreement (*R* v *Siracusa*, 1990)
- a course of conduct that would result in a crime if carried out (*R* v *Jackson*, 1985)

It is also possible to charge conspiracy in connection with any offence.

The *mens rea* is the intention that the crime will be committed. Therefore, it is not a conspiracy where only a conditional consent is obtained (*R* v *Anderson*, 1986), and the fact that the conspiracy is for a good motive does not necessarily negate the *mens rea* (*Yip Chiu-cheung* v *R*, 1994).

Traditionally, impossibility was a defence to conspiracy under the common law. However, s.1(1)(b) of CLA 1977 rules it out for statutory conspiracy and impossibility is treated in the same way as it is in attempt.

Common-law conspiracy

Common-law conspiracy is defined as an agreement by two or more persons to effect an unlawful purpose. It was abolished by s.5 of the **Criminal Law Act 1977**, except in the cases of fraud and public morality. Common-law conspiracy cannot occur between a husband and wife, or with a child under 10 years of age, or, indeed, with the victim of the offence. Impossibility is a defence to common-law conspiracy (*DPP* v *Nock*, 1978).

There are two main areas of common-law conspiracy:

- a conspiracy to defraud (*Scott* v *Metropolitan Police Commissioner*, 1975). This often involves abusing a position of trust (*Adams* v *The Queen*, 1995), and dishonesty is a requirement (*R* v *Wai Yu-Tsang*, 1991).
- a conspiracy to corrupt public morals. This originated in the case of *Shaw* v *DPP* (1962) (the 'ladies directory' case). The case received extensive criticism for the justifications given by the House of Lords in creating what was a new offence. The justification was simply that the House had the power to invent the offence since its members are the 'guardians of public morality'. While the House excused the case as a one-off, a subsequent charge of conspiring to outrage public decency was accepted in *Knuller* v *DPP* (1973). This caused further controversy but prosecutions are still possible (*R* v *Gibson and Sylverie*, 1990).

Conspiracy with a foreign element

This kind of conspiracy obviously depends on jurisdiction. An agreement made in England and Wales is only triable if the offence itself is also triable. It includes murder, even if carried out abroad, and, since the **Criminal Justice Act 1993**, conspiracy to steal, defraud, blackmail, or forge abroad. A conspiracy made abroad to murder in the UK is triable (*DPP* v *Doot*, 1973), and in *R* v *Sansom* (1991) it was suggested that the same could apply to other crimes, but this is not yet settled.

Attempts

An attempt is where the defendant has the necessary criminal intent and sets out to commit the crime but actually fails to complete it. The definition in s.1(1) of the **Criminal Attempts Act 1981** states:

> ...if with an intent to commit an offence to which this section applies, the person does an act which is more than merely preparatory to the commission of the offence, he is guilty of attempting to commit the offence...

A charge of attempt is not possible in the case of summary offences, nor can there be an attempt to conspire, aid, abet, counsel or procure.

One area that proved controversial for a while was the area of 'attempting the impossible'. Under s.1(2) of the Act: 'A person may be guilty of attempting to commit an offence...even though the facts are such that the commission of the offence is impossible.' This overruled a previous unsatisfactory common-law rule that made an attempt that was a legal or factual impossibility beyond prosecution (*Haughton* v *Smith*, 1973).

The section originally caused some difficulty of interpretation for the courts but was eventually resolved correctly by the House of Lords in *R* v *Shivpuri* (1987), which overruled its incorrect interpretation of the previous year in *Anderton* v *Ryan* (1986).

Section 1(3) also clarifies the issue:

> In cases where, apart from this subsection, a person's intention would not be recognised as having amounted to an intent to commit an offence, but if the facts of the case were as he believed them to be, his intention would have been so regarded, then...he shall be regarded as having an intent to commit that offence.

Attempts and the *actus reus*

Under the **Criminal Attempts Act 1981**, the key element of the *actus reus* is that the act is 'more than merely preparatory to the commission of the offence'.

This obviously requires interpretation. Originally there were a number ways of establishing this under the common law. At one time, the test was merely one of proximity (*Comer* v *Bloomfield*, 1970). It was also often measured by the 'last act test' (*R* v *Eagleton*, 1855). A simple test was whether the defendant had reached 'a point from which it is impossible to return' (*DPP* v *Stonehouse*, 1978). However, under the current law, the defendant need not have committed the last act or reached a point of no return (*A-G's Reference No. 3 of 1992*, 1994). Probably the most satisfactory question to ask is whether the defendant has carried out an act that shows that he or she actually tried to commit the offence, or whether he or she has merely put himself or herself in a position where he or she is ready or equipped to commit the offence (*R* v *Geddes*, 1996).

Nevertheless, the words 'more than merely preparatory' have created many grey areas, as can be seen by comparing the results in *R* v *Gullefer* (1987) and *R* v *Campbell* (1991) with those in *R* v *Boyle and Boyle* (1987) and *R* v *Kenneth Jones* (1990).

Attempts and the *mens rea*

The *mens rea* is normally the same as for the main offence. However, it may require a greater degree of intent (*R* v *Walker and Hayles*, 1990). In attempted murder, for instance, it is necessary to show a higher degree of *mens rea* than in the offence itself. Intention to kill is required for attempted murder — intention to cause grievous bodily harm is not sufficient. A defendant must intend a strict liability offence, even though that in itself would have no *mens rea* (*Alphacell Ltd* v *Woodward*, 1972).

Intention may be inferred from foresight of consequences, where the result in question is virtually certain to occur and the defendant knows this (*R* v *Walker and Hayles*, 1990).

In some instances, recklessness has been accepted as appropriate *mens rea*, despite older authorities maintaining the contrary (*R* v *Khan*, 1990). Certain developments have shown a trend towards a general rule of reckless attempts, although that was never intended (*A-G's Reference (No. 3 of 1992)*, 1994).

Fatal offences against the person

Murder

Murder is a homicide offence and is obviously a result crime (however badly the accused has harmed the victim, if the victim does not die, homicide has not occurred).

Unlike most crimes, murder is still a common-law offence. This is technically important only as an issue in drafting indictments. However, the definition of murder is the one set out by Sir Edward Coke in the seventeenth century and it is arguable whether this is satisfactory today. The elements of the offence from the definition are that a person of sound mind over the age of 10 unlawfully kills a reasonable person actually in being and 'residing under the King's/Queen's peace' with malice aforethought, either expressed by the defendant or implied by law. Formerly the definition also required that the victim should die within a year and a day. This has now been removed as the result of the **Law Reform (Year and a Day Rule) Act 1996**. However, reference must be made to the Attorney General in the case of deaths occurring 3 years or more after the attack, and where the defendant has already been convicted of a lesser offence.

As with all crimes, each separate ingredient of the offence must be proved. All ingredients of the offence except malice aforethought are *actus reus* and apply to all homicides.

Malice aforethought alone is the *mens rea* of murder. If malice aforethought cannot be proved, the offence cannot be murder, even though it involves an unlawful killing.

It is, of course, possible for an accused to avoid conviction because he or she can claim a complete defence that negates either the *mens rea* or the *actus reus*. On certain other occasions, both the *actus reus* and the *mens rea* of murder can be proved, but the accused is able to claim one of the special and partial defences identified in the **Homicide Act 1957** and referred to as 'voluntary manslaughter'. In these instances, even though murder can be proved, if the plea is accepted, the charge is reduced to manslaughter.

Murder is classed at the highest level of wickedness. As a result, on conviction it receives a mandatory life sentence. In contrast, in the case of other homicides there may be discretionary sentencing available to the judge. In recent times, several leading judges, as well as law reformers, have called for the mandatory sentence for murder to be removed and for discretion to be used in imposing a sentence that reflects the crime.

The *actus reus* of murder

There are four aspects to the *actus reus* in relation to murder:
- a description of the perpetrator
- the unlawful killing

- a description of the victim
- the jurisdiction of the court

Coke's definition referred to 'a man of sound memory and the age of discretion'. This merely means that the accused is not mentally incapacitated, and is therefore legally sane, or is too young, i.e. under the age of 10, when criminal intent cannot be formed. This definition refers to women too, as well as to children over the age of 10.

A killing must be unlawful for a homicide to occur. By definition, this means that some killings are lawful, and if a killing has a lawful justification it will not be a criminal offence. Lawful killings include:
- a killing carried out in self defence
- (formerly) where the killing was a lawful capital punishment
- where an enemy alien is killed in time of war (although this does not include a prisoner of war)

The victim of a homicide is described as 'a reasonable person actually in being'. This sounds complex and is due to the archaic language used in the original definition. In simple terms, the issue is whether the victim is a living human being at the time of the alleged killing, i.e. a human being who is recognised in law as being alive. Problem areas can concern when life begins, such as in the cases of *R v Brain* (1834), *R v Senior* (1899) and *A-G's Reference (No 3 of 1994)* (1997). Similar problems arise over the issue of when life ends (although, at this point, the major issue is really causation), e.g. *R v Malcharek* (1981), *R v Steel*, (1981), *R v Blaue* (1975), *R v Adams* (1957), *R v Cox* (1992), *Airedale NHS Trust v Bland* (1993) and *Re A (Conjoined Twins)* (2001).

The requirement that the accused should be 'residing under the King's/ Queen's peace' merely refers to the jurisdiction of the court to try the offence. Jurisdiction is very wide, since an English court may try any UK citizen for a murder that he or she has committed anywhere in the world.

The *mens rea* of murder

The *mens rea* of murder is defined as 'with malice aforethought express or implied'. Again, this definition appears to be complex and confusing, because of the archaic language used in Coke's definition.
- 'Malice' in this context does not refer to the usual dictionary definition of 'spite', and could include even mercy killing (*R v Adams*, 1957).
- 'Aforethought' in this context is not necessarily the same as premeditation, so it can include spur of the moment killings (*R v Church*, 1966).
- Express malice simply means the intention to kill.
- Implied malice is the intention to cause grievous bodily harm (this is defined as meaning really serious harm).

Murder is a crime of specific intent, so recklessness can never be sufficient *mens rea* for it. As we have already seen, the necessary intent can be shown either where there is direct intent or where there is oblique intent.

Direct intent is relatively straightforward, and what must be shown is that the defendant desired the actual consequences. Here, foresight is not really an issue (*R* v *Michael*, 1840). However, as we have already seen, murder can still occur where there is oblique intent, of which foresight of consequences is the traditional measure. It does not matter what consequence the defendant actually desired, as long as it can be shown that the actual consequence was foreseeable. Problems have then occurred in determining the part to be played by foresight. At one time, it was measured objectively (*DPP* v *Smith*, 1961) but this was unsatisfactory, since it seemed to negate the need for *mens rea*, and as a result this was amended in s.8 of the **Criminal Law Act 1967**.

Subsequently, foresight of probable consequences and intent were held to be interchangeable (*R* v *Hyam*, 1974), but again this was clearly unsatisfactory, as well as confusing.

After this, only clear intent was held to be sufficient, and foresight of consequences was identified as being the only evidence from which intention could be inferred (*R* v *Moloney*, 1985).

Now, the House of Lords has accepted a workable definition that intention should not be inferred from foresight unless 'death or serious bodily harm was a virtual certainty' (*R* v *Nedrick*, 1986, approved in *R* v *Woollin*, 1998 HL).

Voluntary manslaughter

Voluntary manslaughter is a general term used to refer to the special and partial defences provided by the **Homicide Act 1957**. The key feature is that murder is being charged and both the *actus reus* and *mens rea* of murder can be proved. The defendant generally has no complete defence available and so a conviction is possible.

However, the defendant is able to claim one of the three special and partial defences made available by the **Homicide Act 1957**. If any of these is successfully claimed, this has the effect of reducing the charge from murder to manslaughter and removing the mandatory life sentence.

The three types of special and partial defence are diminished responsibility (s.2), provocation (s.3) and failed suicide pacts (s.4).

Diminished responsibility

The defence of diminished responsibility came about because of the inadequacies of the M'Naghten rules on insanity. The defence has no basis in common law (as provocation does) but is entirely the creation of statute in s.2 **Homicide Act 1957**. It applies only as a partial defence to murder (unlike insanity, which applies generally to all crimes), and is designed to replace insanity, which was seen as sometimes unjust or unsatisfactory.

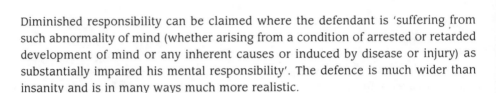

Diminished responsibility can be claimed where the defendant is 'suffering from such abnormality of mind (whether arising from a condition of arrested or retarded development of mind or any inherent causes or induced by disease or injury) as substantially impaired his mental responsibility'. The defence is much wider than insanity and is in many ways much more realistic.

There are three specific elements that must be shown for a successful plea:

- **The abnormality of the mind.** This is determined by the jury, although medical evidence is taken into account. There is no particular definition, although Lord Parker in *R* v *Byrne* (1960) suggested that it was 'a state of mind so different from that of ordinary human beings that a reasonable man would term it abnormal'.
- **The cause of the abnormality.** This must be one of those identified in s.2, which is in fact very wide and covers both internal and external factors. For instance, while ordinary rage would not be sufficient, uncontrollable impulses could be (*R* v *Byrne*, 1960). It could also include abnormality caused by such factors as battered wife syndrome (*R* v *Hobson*, 1997) and severe reactive depression (*R* v *Seers*, 1984), so the list of causes is confusing to psychiatrists as well as to laymen. Drunkenness cannot be a cause, though alcoholism might be (*R* v *Tandy*, 1988). In *R* v *Dietschmann* (2003), the House of Lords identified that drink and the abnormality of mind might both play a part in impairing the defendant's mental responsibility, in which case the jury should determine whether, despite the effect of the alcohol on the defendant's mind, the abnormality still substantially impaired his or her mental responsibility.
- **Substantial impaired mental responsibility.** Again, this is a question of fact for the jury to decide, which can be achieved with very little evidence, or fail where there is a wealth of evidence.

Two significant reforms are suggested in the Draft Criminal Code:

- Intoxication should be kept entirely separate from diminished responsibility.
- The defendant should only have to raise evidence of diminished responsibility and it should then be for the prosecution to disprove it.

Provocation

Provocation was originally a common-law defence and a successful plea depended on actions. Words alone were insufficient to succeed in the defence (*Holmes* v *DPP*, 1946). The common-law definition was 'some act done by the dead man to the accused which would cause a reasonable person and actually does cause the defendant a sudden and temporary loss of control' (Devlin J in *R* v *Duffy*, 1949).

The defence is now found in s.3 **Homicide Act 1957**:

> Where, on a charge of murder, there is evidence on which the jury can find that the person charged was provoked (whether by things done or by things said or by both

together) to lose his self-control, the question whether the provocation was enough to make a reasonable man do as he did shall be left to be determined by the jury...and the jury shall take into account everything according to the effect...it would have on a reasonable man.

The trial judge decides if there is any evidence indicating provocation (*R* v *Acott*, 1997). The judge then leaves the question of whether the defendant was actually provoked to the jury and it is for the prosecution to disprove (*R* v *Cascoe*, 1970).

Members of the jury must ask themselves two questions:

- Was the defendant provoked so that he or she actually lost self-control? (This is the subjective test as in the prior common law, *R* v *Duffy*, 1949.) This should be a sudden and temporary loss of control, so that a cooling off period between the provocation and the loss of control means that the defence is likely to fail (*R* v *Thornton*, 1992 and *R* v *Ahluwalia*, 1992).
- Would a reasonable man have reacted in the same way? (This is the objective question that has proved to be problematic.) This originally caused problems where the defendant had characteristics that the reasonable man would not have (e.g. impotence (*R* v *Bedder*, 1954)). Following *R* v *Camplin* (1978), the age, sex and other relevant characteristics of the accused can be taken into account in determining how the reasonable man would have reacted. Relevant characteristics have been extended to include battered women's syndrome (*R* v *Hobson*, 1997), addiction (*R* v *Morhall*, 1995) and immaturity and attention seeking (*R* v *Humphries*, 1995). However, mental conditions such as brain disorders and depression should not be taken into account, as they are more appropriately dealt with under diminished responsibility (*R* v *Luc Thiet Thuan*, 1997). *R* v *Smith (Morgan James)* (1998) held that abnormal characteristics of the accused may be relevant not only to the gravity of the provocation, but also to the ability of the reasonable man to deal with the provocation. All that the jury should decide is what could reasonably have been expected of the defendant. *R* v *Weller* (2003) confirmed that the test is whether the defendant should reasonably have controlled himself or herself.

Provocation has become an extremely wide defence and almost any characteristic can now be taken into account. It has been argued that *Smith* (1998) reduces the self-control that is to be expected of the defendant to an unacceptably low level. The Law Commission has suggested that either the defence should be abolished or the wording of the section should be changed to:

A person who, but for this section, would be guilty of murder is not guilty of murder if (a) he acts when provoked (whether by things done or said or both and whether by the deceased person or by another) to lose his self-control and (b) the provocation is, in all the circumstances (including any of his personal characteristics that affect its gravity), sufficient ground for the loss of self-control.

The Privy Council in Holley (2005) condemned the Smith test, which is persuasive.

Failed suicide pacts

This is another special and partial defence created by the **Homicide Act 1957**. According to s.4(1): '...it shall be manslaughter, not murder, for a person acting in pursuance of a suicide pact between him and another to kill the other or be a party to the other being killed by a third person.' The defendant must prove the suicide pact and that his acts were done while he or she had 'the settled intention of dying in pursuance of the pact'.

While suicide ceased to be a crime by the **Suicide Act 1961**, it is still unlawful to aid, abet, counsel or procure a suicide or an attempted suicide, making euthanasia more difficult still (*R* v *McShane*, 1977).

The suggestion in the Draft Criminal Code is for 'suicide pact killing' to be an entirely separate offence, rather than a part of manslaughter.

Involuntary manslaughter

Involuntary manslaughter is unlawful killing with insufficient *mens rea* for murder, so it covers those areas where the prosecution is unable to show malice aforethought. In voluntary manslaughter, the defendant did intend to kill or to cause serious harm to the victim, but can claim a special and partial defence provided by statute. In involuntary manslaughter, on the other hand, the defendant is arguing that he or she did not intend to kill, and this is the 'involuntariness' referred to.

However, there is still some measure of culpability, otherwise it would not be an unlawful killing. As a result, involuntary manslaughter is, in some ways, an imprecise area. It can be both complex and diverse as it covers all of those killings which fall between murder and accidental or justified killing. It can also be committed in a number of ways.

Constructive manslaughter (unlawful act manslaughter)

This type of manslaughter is based on the notion of 'constructive malice': if the death occurred during the commission of an unlawful act, the prosecution need only prove *mens rea* of that unlawful act in order to convict for manslaughter. This is why it is also called 'unlawful act' manslaughter.

The major definition was given by Lord Salmon in *DPP* v *Newbury and Jones* (1977), stating that the accused would be guilty of manslaughter if it could be proved that he or she 'intentionally did an act which was unlawful and dangerous and that the act inadvertently caused death'. This approved the judgement of Edmund Davies J in *R* v *Church* (1966): 'the unlawful act must be such as all sober and reasonable people would inevitably recognise and must subject the other person to at least the risk of some harm resulting therefrom.'

The prosecution needs to prove two things, i.e:
- the existence of an unlawful act committed by the defendant
- the unlawful act must be dangerous

The existence of an unlawful act committed by the defendant

An omission would not be sufficient for constructive manslaughter (*R* v *Lowe*, 1973). The act itself must be unlawful rather than a lawful act that has been carried out unlawfully (*Andrews* v *DPP*, 1937), so a death caused by a civil wrong would be insufficient (*R* v *Franklin*, 1883). The unlawful act must be carried out with the appropriate *mens rea* (*R* v *Lamb*, 1967) and there can be no conviction if the act leading to the death was done with lawful justification (*R* v *Scarlett*, 1993). However, intoxication is not an excuse for carrying out an unlawful act that leads to an inadvertent death (*R* v *Lipman*, 1970).

One line of cases that creates apparent difficulties concerns defendants who supply victims with drugs, who subsequently die from taking the drug. The unlawful act identified is usually maliciously administering a noxious substance contrary to s.23 of the **Offences Against the Person Act 1861**. A problem here is proving causation. If the defendant only supplies the drug and does nothing more, there can be no conviction for constructive manslaughter (*R* v *Dalby*, 1982). If the defendant injects the victim, there can be a conviction (*R* v *Cato*, 1976). In *R* v *Kennedy* (1998), it was held that the defendant could be convicted for filling the syringe with which the victim then injected himself, resulting in death, the unlawful act being assisting the victim in his unlawful act. This view, however, was held to be wrong in *R* v *Dias* (2001). In *R* v *Rogers* (2003), an actual act of assisting in the injection, for instance by applying a tourniquet, was found to be an unlawful act that led to a conviction.

The unlawful act must be dangerous

This means that there must be a risk of harm, which reasonable and sober people would recognise as a risk (*R* v *Church*, 1966). There must be a risk of physical harm rather than mere emotional disturbance (*R* v *Dawson*, 1985). However, where a reasonable person would realise that, in the circumstances, the victim's general frailty would lead to a risk of physical harm, there can be a conviction for a resulting death (*R* v *Watson*, 1989). It does not matter that the defendant did not recognise the risk: the test is not 'did the accused recognise that it was dangerous?' but 'would all sober and reasonable people recognise its danger?' (Lord Salmon in *DPP* v *Newbury and Jones*, 1977).

Originally, it was also considered that the unlawful act should be directed at the victim. The original test was that if the unlawful act were only an indirect cause of death, there was no manslaughter (*R* v *Dalby*, 1982). However, this test is outdated and a better test is whether the harm is directly linked to the unlawful act so that it could be aimed at property (*R* v *Goodfellow*, 1986). It is also possible that manslaughter can result from an intentional, unlawful and dangerous act done to another (*A-G's Reference (No 3 of 1994)*, 1997).

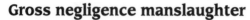

Gross negligence manslaughter

Traditionally, the courts accepted manslaughter caused by gross negligence. This depended first on the defendant owing the victim a duty of care. The original definition was contained in *R v Bateman* (1925):

> ...the facts must be such that...the negligence of the accused went beyond a mere matter of compensation...and showed such disregard for life and safety as to amount to a crime against the state and conduct deserving of punishment...

Gross negligence was distinguished from recklessness in *Andrews v DPP* (1937):

> ...simple lack of care as will constitute civil liability is insufficient...reckless suggests indifference to risk, whereas the accused may have appreciated the risk and intended to avoid it and yet shown such a high degree of negligence in the means adopted to avoid as would justify a conviction...

There was, at one time, a dispute about whether recklessness or gross negligence should be applied and whether the appropriate test ought to be objective or subjective. If the correct test were subjective, then foresight of injury would also be important (*R v Pike*, 1961). However, if the test were objective, then it would be the standards of the jury that should apply (*R v Seymour*, 1983). The House of Lords then accepted the test of objective recklessness from *R v Caldwell* (1982) and *R v Lawrence* (1982) as the appropriate test. This appeared to be the end of gross negligence manslaughter, since Lord Roskill argued that Caldwell recklessness should be applied throughout the criminal law, confirmed again by Lord Roskill in *Kong Cheuk Kwan v R* (1985).

However, there has been a return to gross negligence as a type of manslaughter in *R v Adomako* (1995), where the question was said to be: '...having regard to the risk of death, was the defendant's conduct in the circumstances so bad as to amount to a criminal act or omission...?' There are a further three questions to ask:
- Did the defendant owe the victim a duty of care?
- Did a breach of this duty cause the death?
- If the answer to both the above is yes, was the act or omission amounting to the breach of duty so negligent as to go beyond mere compensation and amount to a crime?

The courts have accepted many situations in which a duty is owed including:
- the duty of a doctor to a patient (*R v Adomako*, 1995)
- the duty of a landlord to a tenant to keep the premises safe (*R v Singh*, 1998)
- a duty arising under a contract where there is an obligation to act (*R v Pittwood*, 1902)
- a duty where the defendant assumes responsibility for the care of another (*R v Stone and Dobinson*, 1977)
- a duty owed by a lorry driver for the safety of illegal immigrants who he knew were hidden in his lorry (*R v Wacker*, 2002)

Misra (2005) states that only the extent to which the breach falls below the appropriate standard is important. It is irrelevant that the act is not illegal in itself.

Gross negligence manslaughter has been criticised for the circularity of the tests involved and also for the use of civil terminology.

Reckless manslaughter

Reckless manslaughter based on the Cunningham model was traditionally available wherever the defendant was aware of a risk and nevertheless carried on to take it, and the taking of the risk resulted in death (*R v Pike*, 1961).

The application of subjective recklessness was denied in both *R v Seymour* (1983) and *R v Lawrence* (1982) at a time when Caldwell objective recklessness was preferred. Prior to *R v Adomako* (1995), the law did recognise the possibility of objective reckless-ness in relation to a charge of manslaughter. In *Adomako* this was held to be wrong, since recklessness should mean that the defendant had been indifferent to the risk of injury, or had foreseen the risk but nevertheless carried on and taken it.

In *R v Lidar* (2000), subjective recklessness appears to have been reintroduced. The case actually concerned an appeal on sentencing. However, the judge, responding to the complaint that the jury had not been directed on gross negligence, identified that this was unnecessary where recklessness was an issue.

Reform of involuntary manslaughter

The Law Commission Report on Involuntary Manslaughter (No 237) in 1996 identified a number of problems with the law on manslaughter:

- the uncertainty of the circumstances in which an omission can lead to liability
- the breadth of the offence which causes difficulties in applying sentences
- the devaluing effect that this can have on more serious examples of the crime
- the fact that manslaughter is 'unprincipled because it requires only that a foresee-able risk of causing some harm' is needed when the defendant is actually convicted of causing death
- the problems associated with the objective character of gross negligence

As a result, the Law Commission has suggested two draft offences:

- **Reckless killing:** where the defendant is aware of a risk that his or her conduct will cause death or serious injury and it is unreasonable for him or her to take that risk in all the circumstances.
- **Gross carelessness killing:** where the risk that the defendant's conduct will cause death/serious injury is obvious to a reasonable person in his or her position, and the defendant is capable of appreciating that risk at all material times. Either his or her conduct falls well below what can reasonably be expected in the circum-stances, or the defendant intends by his or her conduct to cause some injury, or is aware of, and unreasonably takes, the risk that it may do so.

Questions
&
Answers

This section provides you with questions from Section A (essays) and Section B (problems) on the areas of the Unit 2571 specification content covered in this guide and in the style that you will find in the exam. The exam lasts 90 minutes. You will be required to answer one question from a choice of two in Section A, and one question from a choice of two in Section B. All questions are marked out of 50, with 25 marks available for the knowledge that you show (AO1), 20 marks available for your ability to analyse and evaluate the law (essays) or apply the legal principles to factual situations (problems) (AO2), and 5 marks available for your communication skills (AO3).

A-, C- and E-grade answers are provided for each question. The A-grade answers should give you a clear idea of the approach and structure required. They are comprehensive in the knowledge demonstrated and show high-level evaluation or application skills. The C-grade answers have been included to illustrate some of the common problems that result in students achieving lower marks. These answers tend to be quite knowledgeable but do not have the same levels of sophistication in the other skills. E-grade answers are often sketchy with some knowledge shown but not a full appreciation of all the necessary knowledge. They also tend to include some errors of law, and the evaluation or application skills are usually quite poor.

You should not take the A-grade responses as being model answers for you to learn off by heart; the questions in the exam will be different from those presented here. Instead, you should try to give your own answers to the questions first, and then compare them with the answers here to see what you are doing well and where you can make improvements. You will also be able to learn some of the common weaknesses and mistakes made by candidates by reading the C- and E-grade answers and the examiner's comments after them. In this way, you can ensure that you do not make the same mistakes, and that you give fuller answers in the exam in order to obtain a better grade.

Examiner's comments

Each answer is accompanied by examiner's comments, preceded by the icon 🄴. These indicate where credit has been given, recognising the candidate's use of the examinable skills, as explained in the introduction. Section A questions, as well as requiring good AO1 skills of recall of knowledge, also require good essay-writing skills for AO2. Section B questions likewise require good knowledge for AO1 but concentrate on the AO2 skill of application of law. In the C-grade and E-grade answers, the examiner indicates possible improvements that could be made to achieve a higher grade. Remember too the AO3 objective which calls for effective communicative skills, use of appropriate legal terminology and correct spelling, punctuation and grammar.

Question 1

Critically consider whether the law governing involuntary manslaughter is in a satisfactory state.

■ ■ ■

A-grade answer

Involuntary manslaughter involves death where the *mens rea* of murder is not present. There are two major types of manslaughter: constructive act manslaughter (unlawful act manslaughter) and gross negligence manslaughter.

Constructive manslaughter has the same *actus reus* as for murder, i.e. you need to cause death to a human, but there are also three additional *actus reus* elements.

First, there has to be an unlawful act — this has to be an act and not an omission. This is shown in the case of *R* v *Lowe*. In this case there was a neglected child who died. It could not be considered constructive manslaughter as the death was caused by an omission (duty through family relationship).

Second, the act has to be specifically unlawful. *R* v *Lamb* concerns two friends. One of the men shot the other, although both thought that the gun would not fire. Because both defendants did not think it would fire, there was no fear of harm and therefore no assault, so this means that there could be no unlawful act.

The last element is that the act must be dangerous. The case of *R* v *Church* demonstrates this. The defendant attempted to have sex with a woman. When he could not satisfy her, she slapped him, and he then knocked her unconscious. Thinking she was dead, he put her in a river and she drowned. Basically, the act is dangerous if there is a risk of some harm resulting from it. This foresight must be able to be seen by a reasonable and sober person.

R v *Goodfellow* says that the act does not need to be aimed at a person and that it can be aimed at a property, provided that a reasonable, sober person can foresee that it would cause another person at least the risk of some harm.

The case of *R* v *Dawson* involved a robbery of a petrol station. When the elderly attendant pressed the alarm, the defendant fled. Following this, the attendant had a heart attack and died. The defendant's conviction was quashed because he did not know about the attendant's condition. The risk of harm had to be physical and not just fear or apprehension. This case was distinguished by *R* v *Watson*, where the courts said the act became dangerous as soon as the elderly man's frailty became obvious.

The *mens rea* of constructive manslaughter is the *mens rea* of the unlawful act. The defendant does not need to know the act is unlawful and dangerous.

Section A

Gross negligence manslaughter has three elements: duty of care, breach of duty causing death, and gross negligence. There are five common-law duty relationships, but the extent of the term 'duty' is unclear. Examples of duty relationships include duty through contract (*Adomako*), duty through creation of a dangerous situation (*Miller*) and duty through family relationship. Breach applies to where the defendant's conduct has gone below the standards of a normal, sober person. This can be illustrated through the case of *Stone and Dobinson*. The defendants had undertaken to look after their ill relative. The relative died and the defendants were convicted. They had breached their duty. This can be quite harsh, as in this case both defendants had exceptionally low intellect and did attempt to get help. They failed to, due to their lack of ability rather than their lack of care. Their efforts were below the standards of the reasonable person. This is exceptionally harsh and should be modified.

Gross negligence is explained through *Bateman*. In *Bateman* it was said that negligence had to have gone beyond a matter of compensation, showing a distinct lack of regard for life and deserving punishment. This test has been approved in *Adomako* but it is not known how the jury will interpret it.

The current law on involuntary manslaughter has been heavily criticised. The courts' confusion over liability in terms of a negligence-based system of fault or a recklessness-based system of fault has caused instability and a lack of clarity in the law. Due to the case of *Lidar*, there are now three aspects of liability concerning involuntary manslaughter, but given the history of the courts in this area, how long it will last is unknown.

The courts have had problems with defining what constitutes an unlawful act. Cases like *Dias*, *Kennedy*, *Dalby* and *Bland* all show inconsistency and a lack of clarity. There has also been a gap in the existing law and defendants may escape liability. This is demonstrated in *Khan and Khan*. Drug dealers escaped liability because no unlawful act had occurred and there was no duty.

One set of reforms has been suggested by Glanville Williams, who said that gross negligence manslaughter should be abolished, as negligence is not sufficient for a crime as serious as manslaughter.

This area has been looked at a number of times by law reform bodies. In particular, the Law Commission has drafted dramatic changes in this area, calling for a replacement of gross negligence and unlawful act manslaughter. They are to be changed to reckless killing and killing by gross carelessness. These changes represent the current unsatisfactory state of involuntary manslaughter, as they are a dramatic shift from the current law. However, these reforms have not been implemented, so the current unsatisfactory law remains.

e This is a comprehensive answer. The candidate introduces the essay in a succinct manner. There is a strong focus on relevant case law, with the cases being used in an appropriate manner. The candidate supports his/her points well, rather than providing an exhaustive list detailing the case acts. The candidate focuses predominantly on knowledge (AO1) throughout the essay and does not focus on AO2 until the later part of the essay. Although this is satisfactory, some candidates may forget towards the end of the essay to include all the relevant evaluative comments. The only significant criticism of this candidate's work is the limited discussion of the Law Commission's changes. However, the conclusion is commendable for using the question as its focus.

■ ■ ■

C-grade answer

Involuntary manslaughter involves death but the *mens rea* of murder is not present as there is no intent. There are different types of involuntary manslaughter: constructive act manslaughter (also known as unlawful act manslaughter) and gross negligence manslaughter. There is also the element of reckless manslaughter, because without reckless manslaughter there is a gap of liability. This is seen with *Khan v Khan*.

In constructive act manslaughter, there are both *mens rea* and *actus reus* elements. The *mens rea* element is the *mens rea* of an unlawful act. The defendant does not have to know that the act is unlawful and dangerous, as per *Newbury v Jones*.

The *actus reus* elements of constructive act manslaughter are the unlawful act and the fact that the act must be dangerous. The unlawful act has to be an act and not an omission, as per *Lowe*, and it also needs to be unlawful, as per *Lamb*, where it was held that there must be fear of an assault. This is therefore justifying the defendant's actions, which is not satisfactory for the crime, so the law needs to be reformed in this area.

There is then the need for the act to be dangerous, which is an objective test. As in *Church*, the defendant must foresee a risk of harm. It was held that an act must be dangerous if there were an objective risk of some harm, and the risk must be foreseeable by a reasonable and sober person. This was modified by *Dawson*, which allowed the victim's characteristics to be accounted for.

There have been some problems with this. *R v Goodfellows* shows that the act need not be aimed at a person — this is surely justifying the death of someone through a threat that does not directly endanger one's life.

For constructive act manslaughter, the defendant must apply to the rules of causation: he must be the factual cause and the legal cause with no intervening act. The death must also be of a human being.

Gross negligence manslaughter has three elements to it. These are breach of duty of care, breach of duty causing death and gross negligence.

Duty of care is the relationship from omissions. This is signified with *R v Adomako*: when someone fails to perform a contract and it endangers life. It can also be seen with *Stone and Dobinson*. The exact terms of duty are unclear and this part of the law needs reform.

Breach of duty causing death means that the defendant's act has gone below the standard expected of the reasonable, sober person.

For gross negligence it must have gone beyond a matter of compensation, showing a distinct lack of regard for life (as in *Bateman*). This area is in satisfactory state for the governing law body.

The scope of the duty relationship has been criticised, as its application is too narrow.

The area of involuntary manslaughter is in need of reform. One area to be reformed would be to introduce corporate manslaughter to make companies more responsible, as they are currently not taking full responsibility.

Another proposed change is to involve the offences of reckless killing and also killing by gross carelessness. This was proposed in 1994 by the Law Reforms Commission.

e The candidate introduces the area by discussing the difference between murder and involuntary manslaughter. He/she then discusses the current law concerning gross negligence manslaughter and unlawful act manslaughter, outlining the major principles in this area with appropriate case citation. In parts, the candidate makes sporadic comments regarding the effectiveness of certain aspects of the current law. The candidate makes an attempt at the end to focus on AO2 issues, but these are limited and lack development. There is also no conclusion. What the candidate has done is to discuss what he/she knows about the law regarding involuntary manslaughter but has failed to address the set question. He/she has also failed to take into account the blend of AO1 and AO2 and, as a consequence, this would limit considerably the marks available.

■ ■ ■

E-grade answer

Plan
- Good points and bad points
- MR UA broad, D doesn't have to perceive harm
- *Lowe, Lamb, Church, Dawson*

Involuntary manslaughter comes in two types: constructive manslaughter and gross negligence manslaughter. However, reckless manslaughter has been in discussions to come back. There is no *mens rea* for murder to do involuntary manslaughter.

In constructive manslaughter, there are three things you have to comply with. It has to be an act and not an omission, e.g. *R v Lowe*, where a father neglected his child and let it die. The court said there was no act.

Second, the act has to be unlawful. This is seen in *R v Lamb*, where two friends had a gun. They both believed that the gun wouldn't go off. However it did, killing one of the men. The court decided there was no unlawful act, as the men didn't believe the gun would fire.

The act also has to be dangerous. This is seen in a case where a couple went to the bedroom for sex. The man couldn't perform so the woman got angry and slapped him. He hit her, knocking her out. He thought she was dead and dumped her in the river where she drowned. The courts said that this was a dangerous act.

The other type of involuntary manslaughter is gross negligence manslaughter. For this, you have to comply with three sections again. Duty of care is a narrow area and the courts find this very difficult. Breach of the law is where a person has gone below the standard of a reasonable, sober man. Gross negligence is seen in *Bateman*, where a person has gone beyond the matter of compensation, showing a distinct disregard for life, which deserves punishment. The courts have also had difficulties with the concept of an unlawful act.

I don't think that the law governing manslaughter is in a satisfactory state, as the negatives greatly outweigh the positives of the law. One positive factor in involuntary manslaughter is that the *mens rea* is very broad for constructive manslaughter (unlawful act), as the defendant doesn't have to foresee harm to have the *mens rea*, thus making the defence harsher on the defendant. But there are too many problems with it and it should be abolished.

e The candidate sensibly starts off with a plan. Many students, feeling the pressure of available time, immediately jump into questions without fully exploring their demands. A plan is important because it not only allows the candidate to understand the demands of the question, but it also acts as a guide to answering the question. This plan immediately sets the scene for the response and demonstrates the candidate's limited knowledge and poor awareness of the topic area.

In terms of the response, the candidate focuses on the question and tries to use material that addresses it. There is a discussion of the law regarding both unlawful act and gross negligence manslaughter. There is case support for the principles of unlawful act manslaughter, but this is lacking regarding gross negligence manslaughter. Although the candidate cannot remember all the case titles, he/she still attempts to use them, which is a good thing to do. In terms of AO2, the response is extremely basic and only a few comments are made. However, there is a positive attempt to conclude in light of the question.

Question 2

Liability in criminal law normally requires the prosecution to establish that the accused has caused the relevant prohibited consequence or conduct to occur — for instance, in homicide, that the accused has caused the victim's death.

Explain by reference to decided cases how the courts have approached the requirement of causation.

■ ■ ■

A-grade answer

Causation needs to be established by the courts in order to identify the link between the defendant and the result. Causation is a relevant issue in all result crimes, e.g. murder. If the prosecution fails to prove the relevant causation elements, the defendant cannot be liable for that result.

In order to satisfy this, the defendant must be established as the factual and legal cause with no intervening acts. In order for the courts to identify if the defendant is the factual cause of a result, the defendant must satisfy the 'but for' test. This is where a result would not have occurred but for the actions of the defendant. The 'but for' test was not satisfied in *R* v *White*, where the defendant put cyanide in his mother's drink. She died of natural circumstances before she had drunk it and therefore the defendant was not the cause of her death.

The courts then require the defendant to satisfy the legal aspect of causation. This contains two elements. The defendant must be more than the minimal cause of death (with regards to homicide). In the past, the defendant had to be the substantial cause of death; however, this has been altered in the case of *Kimsey*. This case involved the defendant being in a car chase. The car crashed and a passenger died. The courts held that the defendant's driving was more than a minimal or trifling cause of death. This shows distinct modifications in this area. The defendant now only has to be a more than minimal cause rather than a substantial cause. It can be argued that this is too harsh on the defendant. However, it has to be considered that the courts have shown good common sense in this area. They recognise that people should be responsible for their actions. Therefore, the flexibility for the prosecution is significant.

The second legal aspect is that the defendant must accelerate the consequence; for homicide, this means death. The approach to this is established in *R* v *Adams*. This involved a doctor killing his patient. He argued that the patient was terminally ill and was going to die anyway. The courts held that it does not matter if it was by weeks or months, the patient's life was still cut short so the defendant would still be liable. This case has important consequences regarding euthanasia or assisted suicide. It means that you will be a cause of death if you assist in a person's death. It has been argued that this should be changed in order to allow people to die with dignity.

Although you can be the factual and legal cause, you may still not be responsible for the result. This may be due to a factor breaking the chain of causation. However, the courts have been harsh in this area.

A defendant can argue that there was a third party involved, breaking the chain of causation and making him or her not liable as a result. This was argued in *R v Pagett*. A defendant involved in an armed siege used his girlfriend as a shield and shot at the police when escaping. The police returned fire and the girl was killed. The defendant argued that he was not the actual cause of death. However, the court held that the reasonable man could have expected the police to return fire in defence or as an exercise of their duty. Only in extreme circumstances will an intervening act from a third party allow the defendant to escape liability.

The actions of doctors is also an area in which a defendant can argue that he or she was not the cause of death, due to medical negligence. In *R v Smith*, a soldier was stabbed by the defendant twice. The soldier was dropped on the way to hospital, wasn't treated immediately and the doctors failed to notice the wounds in his back. He died shortly afterwards and the defendant appealed due to the bad medical treatment. His appeal was quashed, as the court held that he was still the substantial and operational cause of death. The implications of this case were altered in *R v Cheshire*. This involved the victim being shot and subsequently needing a tracheotomy at hospital. The victim suffered a heart attack due to a side-effect of the tracheotomy. The defendant argued against being the cause of death as the original wounds had healed. The court rejected this and said that only in extreme circumstances will medical negligence break the chain of causation. This is also another indecisive area. This was very unfair on the defendant as the original wounds had healed and the defendant's actions (the gun shot) were not the cause of death. However, public office must be considered and the courts have made sure liability is strong in these areas. An exceptional case, *R v Jordan*, has, however, been distinguished by the courts. The victim was stabbed and received very bad medical treatment and died. The victim's original wounds had healed and the defendant was not convicted, due to the negligent medical treatment. This case is considered to be unique. It is therefore difficult for medical negligence to break the chain of causation. Is this appropriate, especially in cases where the original or operating injury has healed and it is some unforeseen mistake by the medical profession that causes the consequence?

Defendants have argued that turning off life-support machines breaks the chain of causation. The courts' approach to this is established in *Malcherek and Steel*. The courts held that it would be ridiculous and bizarre to allow this to break the chain. This is a common sense approach by the courts — it would be ridiculous in situations of brain death that a defendant is removed from responsibility purely because a doctor has switched off a life-support machine.

Actions of the victim can also be argued to break the chain of causation by the defendant's fright or flight aspect. This is known as the 'daftness test'. This is where the response of the victim is so daft or unexpected that the reasonable man could not expect it. This is shown in *R* v *Williams and Davis*. A hitchhiker jumped out of a moving car and died after the defendants tried to rob him. The court decided his reaction was unexpected and could not have been foreseen. This is a strange aspect of causation. This test is sympathetic to the defendant. Why should defendants like Williams and Davis be absolved from liability because a defendant does something unexpected or unforeseen? Is it reasonable to expect a person to act rationally when being attacked? How would a defendant know that the criminal act being performed would not spiral to other worse criminal acts? The daftness test is indeed daft and needs to be removed.

Self-negligence is also another harsh area for the defendant, e.g. *R* v *Holland*. The defendant cut the victim's finger with an iron bar during a dispute. The victim then sought medical advice and was told that there was a need to amputate the finger. This advice was ignored and the victim developed lockjaw and died. The defendant was still held responsible for the victim's death. This is a highly unfair area on the defendant. Defendants must take victims as they find them and their conditions cannot be used as an excuse. For example, you have brittle bones. I punch you and it causes more damage than normal. This is not an excuse for the defendant, as defendants have to take victims as they find them. This applies to beliefs as well as to physical conditions, as seen in *R* v *Blaue*.

Causation has therefore been developed through the common law on a case-by-case basis. It is a cornerstone of all result crimes and therefore it is of extreme importance. Largely, the courts have developed the rules against the defendant, in that if you have started a chain of events, you will be ultimately responsible. Although this has been argued to be too harsh on the defendant, the courts have had strong public policy considerations. This area has shown the courts to have great common sense, as defendants would try to argue they were not liable for frivolous reasons, e.g. the victim was not given the best medical treatment.

e The candidate starts with a good introduction, setting the scene for the essay, then goes on to discuss the relevant legal principles regarding causation. These principles are supported by good and accurate case citation, with case facts used as explanation rather than just being listed. The candidate covers a significant amount of case material in the time available. Evaluation is interwoven into the answer. The vast majority of legal principles are discussed. The candidate also highlights a number of merits and defects. Importantly, the candidate gives a balanced discussion — most candidates focus too heavily on defects. There is a strong conclusion, which provides an evaluative summary.

■ ■ ■

C-grade answer

Causation is the link between the defendant and the result. If the defendant is to be responsible for the result, the chain of causation must not be broken. If in certain circumstances it is broken, the defendant will not be responsible for the result. It is the prosecution's responsibility to show that the defendant was the factual and legal cause, without an intervening act.

In order to satisfy the factual cause, the 'but for' test is used, i.e. but for the defendant's actions, the result would not have happened. If the defendant doesn't satisfy the 'but for' test, he/she did not cause the result. In *R v White*, a son put cyanide in his mother's drink intending to kill her, but she died of natural causes before she drank the drink. Therefore, he failed the 'but for' test and so wasn't guilty of murder.

The legal cause states that the defendant must accelerate death. *R v Kimsey* changed the law from the defendant being a substantial cause to being more than minimal cause. In the case of *R v ?*, a doctor argued that he hadn't killed his patient because the patient was already dying. However, the courts said that it didn't matter if life was shortened by even a few seconds, it is still murder. The courts have stated that the defendant doesn't have to be the main or sole cause of the result.

Actions of the victim or a third party can, in certain circumstances, break the chain of causation. *R v Paggett* involved the defendant using his girlfriend as a shield to police fire after he shot at the police. She died and his appeal was dismissed because it was reasonably foreseeable that the police would fire back.

There have been cases that forced the courts to clarify the issue surrounding actions of a doctor where a defendant inflicted an injury but argued that he/she didn't cause the result due to medical negligence. *R v Cheshire* overruled the previous case of *R v Smith* by saying that only in extreme circumstances would medical negligence break the chain of causation. However *R v Jordan* is an exception to this rule because the defendant was found not guilty due to the fact that the original wounds had healed and the medical treatment was extremely poor. But there are problems with the case because it has been described as unique and is therefore easier to distinguish. When considering causation, the action of the victim is considered. For the defendant to be liable he/she must fail the 'daftness test', which states that the victim must do something so daft that no reasonable person could foresee it. *R v Williams and Davis* shows that the defendants were found not guilty after the hitchhiker they tried to rob died after jumping from their car. The jury wasn't told to consider the victim's response. In *R v Marjoram*, the defendants were found guilty because the result was foreseeable. The defendant cannot use self-neglect as an intervening act. *R v Blave* showed that defendants must take their victims as they find them. In *Blave*, the defendant refused a blood transfusion on religious grounds.

e This response provides an overview on the major elements of causation and the candidate clearly has a grasp of the major cases involved. However, some cases are lacking titles or are spelt incorrectly, e.g. *R v Blave* instead of *R v Blaue*. The knowledge demonstrated is of a good standard, showing understanding of the key themes and concepts. What this candidate fails to do is to develop these materials by evaluating and discussing them. There is a lack of comment, and when it is made, it is not sufficiently developed. The candidate's AO2 mark would, therefore, be low. The candidate has also failed to reach a conclusion, which is a key to achieving marks at the higher end of the marking criteria.

E-grade answer

Causation is part of the *actus reus*. It applies to consequence crimes. Have to be factual and legal cause. Factual is the but for test, *White*, and legal is tests that have to be satisfied, e.g. acceleration test for murder.

Sometimes issues break chain of causation. *Williams and Davis* and *R v Marjoram*. The victim must fail the daftness test for the defendant to be found not guilty. If the victim does something so stupid that the defendant would never have foreseen it at all, the defendant would not be liable as seen in *Williams and Davis* when a hitchhiker jumped out of a moving car to avoid being robbed. In *Marjoram*, however, the victim's actions were seen as reasonably foreseeable after the victim jumped out of a window after his room was broken into. The matter of 'reasonably foreseeable' is one for the jury which could lead to inconsistencies as different juries would decide different things.

Self-neglect can be seen in the case of *R v Holland* where the victim received a cut finger and ignoring medical advice did not treat it. He died and the defendant was convicted despite the victim's actions. This seems particularly harsh on the defendant who did not administer much damage to the victim.

One more rule is that the defendant must have the victim as he finds him or her: for example, if someone has fragile bones, and receives a broken arm after being punched, the defendant cannot use the victim's position as an excuse. This also applies to mental conditions or victim beliefs as well as physical conditions as seen in *R v Blaue*. In *Blaue*, a woman was stabbed and died after refusing a blood transfusion (it was against her religious beliefs), defendant was convicted as he had to take the victim as he found her. This also seems harsh. The courts have modified this area by changing from substantial causes to minimal causes which makes things harder for the defence. The courts have also shown strong common sense by making sure liability is strong in certain areas, e.g. medical treatment, defendant could always complain that he/she should be found not guilty as the victim was not given the best treatment. This is maybe unfair on the defendant as even when an original wound has healed, they can be found guilty.

🖉 This response is disjointed and lacks clarity in parts. The opening paragraph is confused. There is an attempt at an introduction but it is very short and lacks precision. Five cases are mentioned, some of which attempt to blend AO1 and AO2 (e.g. the discussion on *R v Blaue*). However, some cases are just mentioned and not expanded to support or strengthen the AO1 or used as an opportunity to develop AO2. The candidate would have benefited from spending a few minutes at the start to work out a plan, and at the end to proofread the essay in order to maximise AO3 marks.

Question 3

'English law does not, in general, impose liability for a failure to act, despite the fact that there may be compelling moral justifications for doing so. For example, the courts have often explained that there is no legal duty upon a stranger to rescue a drowning child.'

Assess the truth of this statement and consider whether the current principles governing liability for omissions are satisfactory.

■ ■ ■

A-grade answer

An omission is a failure to act — for example, you watch a person drown. In criminal law there is no criminal liability for failure to act, although there are two exceptions. First, there are statutory exceptions, which are normally strict liability offences. An example of this would be refusing to take a breath test, when asked to do so by the police. Second, there are common-law exceptions, and this occurs when the court decides you are under a duty to act.

An omission is part of the *actus reus* for certain crimes, e.g. murder and gross negligence manslaughter. Certain crimes cannot be done via an omission, e.g. unlawful act manslaughter and robbery.

As the question states, English law imposes no general duty on people to help each other out or to save anyone from harm. Therefore, you can watch a drowning child in certain circumstances and have no legal liability. However, the courts will uphold legal liability for a failure to act if there was a duty. There are currently five situations that are duty situations.

Duty through contract is when a person has a positive duty to act due to a contract. It normally arises when a failure to perform your contract endangers life. Therefore, lifeguards and doctors can be held criminally liable for failure to perform their contracts. This was shown in the case of *R* v *Pittwood*, where a gatekeeper of a railway line went for lunch, leaving the gate open. A hay cart crossed the line and was hit by a train. One man was killed and another was seriously injured. The defendant was convicted of manslaughter based on a failure to carry out his contract to close the gate when a train was approaching.

Cases like *Pitwood* and *Adomako* have liability imposed because you are paid to perform a set task and if you fail to perform it you should be responsible. However, academics like Ashworth question the need for criminal liability in these circumstances and think the civil law and compensation are more appropriate than criminal sanctions.

Duty through public office is shown in the case of *R* v *Dytham*, where a uniformed policeman saw a man being kicked to death. The policeman took no steps to intervene and drove away quickly when the violence was over. The defendant was convicted of wilfully, and without reasonable excuse, neglecting to perform a duty to protect the victim. Criminal liability is imposed here because the courts consider that those in positions of public trust should achieve certain standards of behaviour.

Duty from family relationships is shown in *Gibbons and Proctor*. Gibbons was cohabiting with Proctor and all their children. However, one child, of whom Proctor was not the natural mother, was kept separate from the rest and ill-treated by Gibbons. The child starved to death. Gibbons owed the child a duty through family relationship and was convicted. This area is considered so important that it has been placed on a statutory footing.

Assumption of a duty of care is shown above as Proctor was convicted of manslaughter. The idea of duty of care is shown in depth by *Stone and Dobinson*. The husband and wife were of low intelligence. They took Stone's sister into their home, providing her with a bed. However, she became ill. She wasn't fed and she developed bed sores and eventually died as a result of this. The two defendants tried to ring a doctor but were of low intelligence and didn't know how to use a telephone. They were convicted of manslaughter, as the defendants had been under a common-law duty and failed to carry it out.

The case of *Stone and Dobinson* shows how harsh the duties can be on the defendant. People are liable who should not be. The defendants did try to help Stone's sister and did their best considering their low level of intellect. This case does not demonstrate a need for criminal liability via omissions — it is morally unjust that they were convicted and sent to prison.

A duty can also arise when you create a dangerous situation. This is shown in the case of *R* v *Miller*. If you start a situation which results in harm, you are liable if you become aware of the situation and fail to take steps to minimise the harm.

The duty scenarios have been heavily criticised by some people. There appears to be an inconsistency. How can a person of low intelligence be liable, but not a person who watches a child drown? All it would take to discharge would be a phone call.

This area is treated differently in other legal systems. For example, France has a 'Good Samaritan' law, which means that strangers owe a duty of care. The Good Samaritan law makes it an offence not to act in certain circumstances.

This area is inconsistent, as there is no reason why some relationships have arisen and others have not. In addition, why do some occupations have a duty and some do not? The courts have sometimes called a situation that is an omission an act (*Fagan*), and an act an omission (*Bland*). This has not helped this area of the law.

There is a reluctance to form new duty relationships, for example *Khan and Khan* where drug dealers watched as one of their clients died. They were not liable to act as they had no duty to act.

To conclude, there are problems with the law on omissions. This has not been helped by the judiciary, who have developed the law on a case-by-case basis without any logical order or plan. There is a need to review this area systematically but on legal lines, not moral ones. The law can only be shaped on moral lines by Parliament whose members are elected by the people, and it is not for the judiciary to dictate moral boundaries.

📝 This is a very strong response given the time constraints and the pressurised conditions. There is a clear explanation of the legal concepts and principles surrounding this area. The concepts are supported by appropriate case law, with the candidate using a variety of cases and discussing them at an appropriate level.

The candidate makes a range of AO2 points. There is a discussion of the legal principles, not only in terms of the merits and defects of the duty but also regarding the topic as a whole.

The essay has a clear introduction, main body and conclusion. AO3 criteria are well met in this response. The candidate refers and responds to the question throughout, and concludes with the quote in mind.

■ ■ ■

C-grade answer

An omission is a failure to act. In English law there is no duty to act, except in certain situations. These situations have been created both buy [sic] statutes and common law. The main ones made by statutes are strict liability offences, such as failure to provide a police officer with a breath sample. There are more omission situations created by Parliament than by judges, which shows Parliament is more at ease when creating omission-based crimes. Most omission situations created by Parliament are regulatory with a minimal punishment and are created to uphold public policies.

The common-law situations occur when the court decides you have a duty to act. There are five duty relationships created by the courts. The first is duty through contract. This is where a failure to perform the contract endangers life, such as doctors, lifeguards etc. This enforces high standards in life-threatening jobs. However, it does not cover situations such as where teachers could teach a class the wrong thing and then they fail their exams which could ruin someone's life.

In R v Adomako, an anaesthetist was convicted of manslaughter because he failed to notice that a breathing tube had come disconnected during the operation.

You could also have a duty through family relationships. This is shown in Gibbons and Proctor. The father of a number of children kept one child separate and starved her to death. It was decided that Gibbons owed her a duty of care because he was the father. The government decided this was such an important issue that they past [sic] a statute covering it.

The third duty is where you assume a duty of care. In the case of *Gibbons and Proctor*, Proctor, Gibbons's lover, was also convicted because she assumed a duty of care.

However, this has been taken to the extreme in *Stone and Dobinson*. The defendants was [sic] of low intelligence and looking after an elderly sister. The defendants tried to get help but was [sic] too thick to contact anyone. The sister died and the defendant was convicted of manslaughter. This is very harsh as the defendant had tried to get help but had been unable. This does not fit with *Khan and Khan*.

There is also a duty through public office and this is shown in *R v Dytham*. A police officer witnessed a violent attack on the victim by two doormen. He took no steps to intervene and was convicted of wilfully and without reasonable excuse neglecting to perform a duty.

There is also a duty when you create a dangerous situation. If you create a situation that results in harm, you are liable if you become aware of the situation and fail to take steps to minimise the harm. This is shown in *R v Miller*.

The duty is ended when it has been communicated to the parties or if the act is futile.

e This essay covers the major issues and themes regarding omissions. The introduction, which focuses on the difference between parliamentary and common-law omissions, is good and demonstrates strong awareness of the area.

The weakness of this response is the main body of the essay. Although it outlines the main duty relationships, there is inconsistent detail regarding the legal principles and cases. Some areas are discussed and developed but others lack depth, e.g. the explanation regarding dangerous situations.

AO2 is limited. The comments are not developed or explained fully, e.g. the elaboration on *R v Stone and Dobinson* states that the decision was harsh and then a link is made to *R v Khan and Khan* but it is not explained. It is critical to discuss aspects of the law.

The question also lacks a conclusion and fails to address the question fully. There are frequent mistakes in grammar and spelling that would affect the AO3 mark, e.g. 'buy' in paragraph 1, 'past' in paragraph 4 and the use of a singular verb in paragraph 6. It is essential to read through your answers to correct such errors.

■ ■ ■

E-grade answer

Plan
Common law duty — 5 situations
Negatives
Harshness — Stone + Dobinson
Reluctance — Khan + Khan
Samaritans
Inconstancies [sic]

Positive

8 covers a gap

1998 Offences Against The Person Act create assault by omission

It is true that English law does not impose liability for a failure to act. However, there are two kinds of exceptions to this, statutory exceptions and common-law exceptions. Statutory exceptions are normally offences that carry a strict liability, e.g. failing to stop at a red light. Then there are common-law exceptions which are created by judges. These actually occur when courts have created a 'duty friendship' which says that because of your position or relationship with the victim, you should have acted. The already established relationships are:

- duty through contract — when failure to perform a contracted job endangers life. This was seen in *Adomako* when an anaesthetist didn't fit a breathing pipe sufficiently and the patient died.
- duty from family relationships — this was seen in *Gibbons and Proctor* when one child was kept separate from a number of others and starved to death.
- assumption of duty — when you take responsibility for someone else, as in *R v ...*
- public office — when someone who works in public office fails to perform a duty. Like the negligent policeman.
- creating a dangerous situation.

This area has also seen a reluctance to create more duty relationships. Omissions have been labelled as quite harsh on the defendant.

e The candidate starts with a plan, which is always a good idea. It covers material not mentioned in the main body of the essay for which the candidate should be given some credit.

The essay starts with a good introduction providing an overview of the law regarding omissions. It then lists the duty areas and discusses them to a varying degree. Some aspects are listed and others are developed with case support. Unfortunately, under the bullet point for assumption of duty, the candidate has forgotten the case of *R v Stone and Dobinson*.

The AO2 is covered more in the plan than in the main body and lacks development.

The style of response suggests a timing issue. Although this bullet-point approach is not ideal, it can be a way of showing the examiner that you understand the material that should be covered. In terms of AO3, the grammar is poor.

Question 4

Critically evaluate the effectiveness of the defence of diminished responsibility. You should refer to both legislation and decided cases in your answer.

■ ■ ■

A-grade answer

Diminished responsibility (DR) is one of the partial defences available to individuals who have committed murder, as it reduces their sentence from murder to manslaughter. The positive effect of this is that it gives the judge flexibility when sentencing, as the options range from an absolute discharge to life.

The procedure regarding DR is that the defendant bears the burden of proving the defence on the balance of probabilities. If the defendant pleads guilty to manslaughter on the basis of DR, it is up to the judge to accept this.

It is only a partial defence because it does not result in a full acquittal and the defence can only be used for the offence of murder. DR is the most popular defence used for murder and is used in 80% of cases. The area is covered by the s.2(1) Homicide Act 1957. The definition in s.2(1) regarding DR can be split into three elements.

The first element is that the defendant must have an abnormality of the mind. The definition of abnormality is very wide, although the condition must be recognisable and the defendant must obtain medical evidence from an expert to support his claim. Whether the defendant has an abnormality of mind is a matter for the jury. This creates a problem, as different juries will perceive abnormality differently. As a whole, abnormality is seen as a mind state so different from that of a normal human being that a reasonable man will perceive it to be abnormal.

An abnormality of the mind was shown in the case of *Byrne*, who was a sexual psychopath and had sexual desires that he couldn't control. He killed a girl in a hotel and mutilated her body. His conviction was reduced from murder to manslaughter.

The second element is that the abnormality of the mind must have come from a substantial cause. There are four parts to this and the defendant must prove one. The four are: a condition of arrested and retarded development, any inherent cause, induced by disease or induced by injury. The range of issues covered under this element is very wide as it includes mental and physical diseases, depression, epilepsy and conditions brought about due to blows to the head. It can therefore be easy for the defendant to satisfy one of these elements.

The above two elements are rather easy to prove for a defendant, because as long as he/she can prove with evidence that he/she has an abnormality of the mind (which is very wide) which has come from a specified cause (where there is a range of options), then the defendant is two-thirds of the way to using the defence.

The third element is that the abnormality of the mind must substantially impair mental responsibility. This means that it must have affected the mind-state to such an extent that it caused the person to commit the crime. However, the abnormality does not have to be the total reason for why the defendant committed the crime, but it has to be substantial. 'Substantial', according to Lloyd, does not mean total and it does not mean trivial. It is somewhere in between and an issue for the jury. Hence, DR is rather easy to prove, which possibly explains why it is used in 80% of all defence to murder cases.

DR is also linked to intoxication. There are two different scenarios in this area. If the defendant kills whilst intoxicated and whilst having an abnormality of the mind, it will be unlikely that you can use DR as the defence. However, if the defendant kills due to the abnormality of the mind, and is just intoxicated at the time, the alcohol will be taken into account and so the defence could be used. The first scenario was shown in *Gittens* where the defendant got drunk, took pills and then killed his wife and strangled his daughter. The Court of Appeal (C of A) noted that the jury should ignore the fact that the defendant was intoxicated and should focus purely on whether he had an abnormality of the mind. The second scenario occurred in the case of *Tandy*. Tandy was an alcoholic and drank a drink she didn't normally have. She killed her daughter. The C of A noted that the alcohol could be taken into account when using the defence.

However, there are also some problems when looking at DR as a defence. The Butler Committee believed that the whole defence of DR should be abolished and just used as a mitigating factor in relation to murder. However, the Law Revision Committee stated that this would lead to the offence of murder being too wide and that the jury would be reluctant to find the defendant guilty, if elements of DR are involved.

Other disadvantages include the fact that the link it has with provocation takes medical characteristics into account and therefore most defendants plead DR and provocation and insanity. However, insanity is not popular with defendants due to the social stigma attached to it.

It has also been argued that the burden of proof should be placed on the prosecution. This has perceived problems for the prosecution in proving that the defendant was not suffering from DR.

The final problem is that all of the law is not covered by the Homicide Act 1957, and that, on some occasions, the judges have had to create common law. This case-by-case development has seen a blurring between provocation and diminished responsibility.

🖉 The essay demonstrates a strong grasp of the law regarding diminished responsibility throughout. It starts with a good explanation of the basis for the defence and the mechanics of its operation. It then breaks s.2(1) into three elements and explains them using appropriate citation. This is a good methodical approach. Although some cases are not covered, most notably *Dietschman*, this does not affect the AO1 significantly.

AO2 comments are concentrated at the end of the essay, although the candidate has made some comments in the main body of the response. These comments are mainly the more obvious points and are not fully developed.

In terms of AO3, the work is logical and although it is sometimes rather clumsily expressed, this does not detract from the overall answer. The essay does, however, lack a formal conclusion addressing the question, which could have ensured more marks.

■ ■ ■

C-grade answer

The defence of diminished responsibility (DR) is covered in s.2 of the Homicide Act. s.2(1) has three essential elements, which are: an abnormality of the mind, arising from certain specified causes, which substantially impairs mental responsibility.

Abnormality of the mind is an issue for the jury. The case of *Byrne* gives an example of this. The defendant was a sexual psychopath who found it impossible to resist his desires. He strangled a girl and mutilated her body. He was convicted of manslaughter. The court stated that abnormality of the mind meant a state of mind so different from a normal human being that the reasonable man would see it as abnormal. This is a very wide definition.

There are several types of specified causes: a condition of arrested and retarded development, e.g. mental deficiencies, any inherent cause (not necessarily something genetically inherited), or the following have been accepted as inherent causes — psychopathy, paranoia, epilepsy, depression, pre-menstrual tension.

The third element is substantially impairing mental responsibility. The case of *Lloyd* noted that substantial does not mean total, nor does it mean trivial, but it is between these. Because of this, it is left to the jury to decide.

Another area of DR is intoxication. For this area, there are two situations to consider. In the first situation, the intoxication does not support the DR claim. If a defendant falls into the second situation, then the intoxication can be taken into account.

In the case of *Tandy*, the defendant was an alcoholic. She got drunk on a type of alcohol she did not normally drink, and she then murdered her daughter. It was stated that if the alcoholism reached a level at which the brain was injured, then the defence was available, but the drinking must be involuntary. For this reason, the defendant was convicted of murder and her appeal was unsuccessful. The jury has to believe it is the abnormality and not the intoxication that caused the defendant to kill, although the alcohol can still be taken into account.

There are problems with the defence of diminished responsibility. One problem is that medical evidence is critical to DR and without the defect it is likely to fail. It also needs to be a recognised condition.

There are overlaps between the defences of DR and insanity, and this can result in the prosecution raising the defence of insanity in response to a claim of DR. However, the defence of insanity is not popular with defendants.

It does seem that the defence of diminished responsibility is fairly effective and works well in most cases. However, there does seem to be some confusion when it comes to there needing to be a clear definition.

e This essay has a positive awareness of the principles and issues surrounding diminished responsibility. In comparison with the A-grade response, it does not support these principles with appropriate case citation. For example, the comparison of diminished responsibility and intoxication in this essay gives only a brief insight into the issues. The A-grade response has better explanation in this area.

The AO2 is also of a lower level. Although it shares the same style as that of the A-grade response, the AO2 comments lack depth and sophistication.

In terms of AO3, this work has a solid structure with an introduction, a developed main body and a valid conclusion.

■ ■ ■

E-grade answer

The defence of DR is one of three partial defences available for murder charges and it can reduce murder to manslaughter. DR is covered under s.2 of the Homicide Act 1957. It is said that for the defence to succeed, the defendant must prove that he had an abnormality of the mind arising from specific causes that substantially impairs mental responsibility.

Arising from specified causes means any related deficiencies, due to injury, or disease such as epilepsy and paranoia. Medical evidence is crucial and will strengthen the case. It must be a recognised disease and it is down to the defendant to plead his condition.

There are problems with DR and intoxication.

The defence of DR is difficult for the courts and the jury to comprehend, especially in complex cases. The trouble is that the defence borders very closely, and even overlaps in some cases, with insanity. This has brought confusion in the courts. Where the defendant pleads DR, the prosecution would try and raise insanity because the risk of being sectioned to an asylum is a scary thought.

The defence's effectiveness works well. Criticisms have been made to the procedure where perhaps the defendant should be required to be tested by two doctors to establish a clear view of the defendant's condition. It has been shown by a number of studies that the procedure, as it stands, is flawed, where the defendant is allowed to bring in his or her own doctor with extensive qualifications to say that the defendant has an abnormality of the mind and then the defence succeeds. The reason is that the jury will believe the doctor with the most qualification, their peers someone higher in authority they will believe him because of the authoritarian principle described by a psychologist, Freud. Many have asked that the defence be scrapped or that it is available to all offences. The defence so far can be flawed and is easily issued. Perhaps there should be greater tests to be passed and more criteria to be fulfilled.

Medical evidence is critical to DR. Without medical support, it is likely that the defence will fail. It also needs to be a recognised condition.

The Butter Committee and the Criminal Law Revision Committee wanted DR changed.

The blur between DR and insanity has created an overlap between them. This can result in the prosecution raising the defence of insanity in response to a claim of DR. Insanity is not popular with defendants.

There is a basic awareness of the principles governing diminished responsibility. However, the principles lack elaboration. This candidate needed to discuss a greater range of issues and support these points with citation, e.g. Byrne, Gittens etc.

The response has a range of AO2 comments ranging from bald statements concerning the problems of diminished responsibility and intoxication, to more detailed development of the individual problems. With a bit more depth and detail, this work could easily move up the mark bands, e.g. by adding a detailed discussion of the reforms suggested by the Butler Committee.

In terms of AO3, the fifth paragraph in particular is muddled. This candidate could have earned more marks by reading through and correcting the answer.

Question 5

Stuart, a reformed heroin addict who has not taken any heroin for 2 months, is sitting in a café having a quiet drink. Hannah, an acquaintance from his drug-taking past, sees Stuart and comes over to where he is reading a newspaper. Hannah knocks the paper out of his hand and says: 'Fancy meeting you here, you old junkie.'

Stuart, who is well known for having a short temper, merely responds by picking up the paper from the floor and replying: 'What do you want?' 'I want to score some heroin from you,' Hannah responds. Stuart replies that he has kicked the habit months ago. Hannah says: 'You lying rat, you'll never be able to quit the habit; everyone knows you're a waster and a slave to drugs.' Stuart, who is in fact still suffering from heroin withdrawal symptoms, which sometimes affect his behaviour, says: 'It's true I've packed it up, now shove off!' Disgusted by this, Hannah throws the remainder of her drink in Stuart's face. Enraged, Stuart takes out a knife and stabs Hannah, killing her instantly. Stuart has now been charged with murder.

Discuss Stuart's potential liability, taking into account any defences that may be available to him.

■ ■ ■

A-grade answer

This scenario involves murder, and the defence of provocation and possibly DR, which could reduce the conviction from murder to manslaughter.

To be guilty of murder, the defendant must have caused the death of another human being, in a country of the realm, under the Queen's peace. There must also be malice aforethought, the *mens rea* element of murder, which is intention to cause death or GBH.

In this scenario, Stuart has obviously fulfilled the *actus reus* of murder and it is very likely that the jury will find the relevant *mens rea*. Even if Stuart argues he did not intend to kill, the *mens rea* of murder includes intent to cause GBH. Taking a knife and stabbing someone is clearly intent to cause GBH as a minimum. If he were convicted of murder, Stuart would receive a life sentence. However, if he successfully used the defence of provocation or diminished responsibility (DR), he would reduce the conviction to manslaughter and could potentially receive a lesser sentence.

Provocation is covered by s.3 of the Homicide Act. To use this there must be things done or said (as per *Doughty and Pearson*). Hannah has obviously done something (she threw a drink in his face) and said something, as she has made a number of abusive comments.

The defendant must have also lost his self-control. The test for this is outlined in *Duffy*, which states the loss of self-control must be sudden and temporary. There are a number of incidents in a short space of time. According to Humphreys, it does not have to be the last act. Given that Stuart stabs Hannah in an enraged state, it is highly likely that he will satisfy this element, but it is an issue for the jury.

The stumbling block may be the 'reasonable man test', where the jury has to decide if the reasonable man with the defendant's characteristics would have lost his self-control. The lead case for this is *Smith,* which allows the jury to take into account characteristics of the defendant. However, these characteristics are limited in the case of *Camplin*. Excluded characteristics are exceptional excitabilities, ill temper or drunkenness. In terms of Stuart, his age and sex and the withdrawal from the heroin could be taken into account, but his short temper would be excluded. It is then up to the jury to decide if the reasonable man with the defendant's allowed characteristics would have lost his self-control. If this is accepted, the defendant would be able to use the defence of provocation.

For the defence of provocation to be used in the first place, the judge must decide if there is sufficient evidence for the defence to use. This is very likely in this case. If the judge allows provocation to be argued, then it is up to the prosecution to prove beyond all reasonable doubt that there is no provocation. This means that, if there is any doubt in the jury's mind, provocation must be allowed.

To use diminished responsibility then, there must be an abnormality of the mind. This is a state of mind so different from that of a normal human being that the reasonable person would term it abnormal, as decided in the case of *Byrne*. In this case, it is up to the jury to decide whether Stuart may have a defect of the mind caused by the heroin withdrawal.

The abnormality of the mind must have come from a specified cause. There are four specified causes, but none really cover withdrawal or addiction. His drug addiction may have caused depression, or the drug addiction could have caused some physical harm to the brain. Stuart therefore may be able to satisfy this element of DR.

The abnormality of the mind must substantially impair the defendant's judgement. In the case of *Lloyd*, it was stated that substantial does not mean total, but it also does not mean trivial. Again, it is up to the jury to find, but as it is very wide then it is quite easy to pass.

It is up to the judge whether to allow DR to be put to the jury, but the burden of proof rests with Stuart. It is also important that Stuart can bring medical evidence of any condition — without it, his claim for DR will most likely be rejected.

Stuart is highly likely to satisfy the *actus reus* and *mens rea* of murder. He can raise the defence of both provocation and diminished responsibility and it does not matter that he tries to use both. There are merits to both issues and it is likely that he may be successful. The crucial issue for both is the belief of the jury.

📝 The candidate starts with a brief but appropriate introduction, outlining the major issues. This is a good way to start a problem question.

The response goes on to identify any potential liability regarding Stuart. Again, this is a good style to adopt. The answer then quickly, but correctly, identifies the major elements of murder. It does not spend too much time on elements that are clearly identified. The candidate uses appropriate elements from the question to support his/her conclusions, e.g. the discussion surrounding malice aforethought.

An insightful analysis of the defences of provocation and diminished responsibility is given. Case law is used but it is not discussed in detail. This is a correct approach, although sometimes it is appropriate to explain more regarding a case when it has similarities with the scenario. The candidate then makes informed judgements about the law in relation to the question. In certain parts, he/she gives a neutral response, such as 'it will be an issue for the jury'. This can be a valid approach if there is uncertainty as to the liability of a defendant to an aspect of the law.

There is a good blend of law and its application throughout. The response is based firmly on the question, and the use of the question to aid the answer is commendable. There is a logical order and elements are discussed in turn. AO3 is very strong.

■ ■ ■

C-grade answer

Stuart may be liable for murder. For him to be liable for murder, he must satisfy the *actus reus* and *mens rea*. For the *actus reus* (AR) to be satisfied, he must be the cause of death, it must be the death of another human being, under the Queen's peace, within a year and a day and within any country of the realm.

📝 The candidate is discussing outdated law. The year-and-a-day rule has been removed. Candidates are expected to know the law as it stands 1 year before the exam.

Stuart must also satisfy the *mens rea* (MR). For this, Stuart must have intended to kill the victim, i.e. he needed malice aforethought. In this instance, there was direct intent present, which means that Stuart has both the AR and MR of murder and so is liable for it.

There are two partial defences that Stuart could consider, as he could not use the suicide pact. These come under the Homicide Act 1957 and are sections 2 and 3.

For the defence of provocation, in s.3 of the Homicide Act there are three elements that need to be satisfied: things done or said, loss of self control and whether the reasonable man would have lost his self-control.

For things done or said, there is a wide area of acceptance in Stuart's case. He would satisfy this first element, as his action was a direct result of the provocative conduct.

The second element is loss of control, which means loss of temper. *Duffy* states that it must be sudden and temporary, which in Stuart's case it was, although it would be up to the jury to decide this. *Ibram* reinforces *Duffy*, although the case of *Thornton* shows that the loss of self control wasn't in front so she was not allowed the defence of provocation.

ℓ This part of the answer is not expressed well. What is the meaning of 'wasn't in front'?

For the 'reasonable man test', the objective test is 'would the reasonable person of the same characteristics have been provoked and would he have acted in the same way?' *Camplin* allowed the age and sex of the defendant to be taken into account.

In Stuart's case, it would be up to the jury to decide if the defence of provocation could be used.

The ulterior defence would be diminished responsibility according to section 2 of the Homicide Act 1957. There are three elements to the defence of DR, and all of these need to be satisfied.

The defendant must be suffering from an abnormality of the mind, but this has a very wide definition, as per *Byrne*. However, medical evidence is needed, as it is likely the defence will fail. This may be satisfied due to Stuart's withdrawal symptoms.

The second element is specified cause, which can be anything from a condition of arrested and retarded development, any inherent cause induced by disease or induced by injury.

The third element is that the abnormality substantially impairs: it doesn't have to be total nor trivial as per *Lloyd*, so the defendant can have awareness.

However, the defence of DR is not really a viable alternative as there is a lack of medical evidence and the defence of provocation seems more likely in this instance.

ℓ The answer focuses immediately on the critical aspects of the question. There is a discussion regarding murder and the candidate touches on the elements of the offence. The candidate then states that Stuart satisfies these elements. It would have been beneficial to discuss this in slightly more detail. For example, the section of the A-grade answer regarding malice aforethought would gain AO2 marks for the discussion and then extra AO2 marks for the application of the law.

There is a reasonable discussion regarding provocation. Certain key cases are omitted, e.g. *Smith*, regarding the objective element. The candidate should then have used this information to greater effect by applying it to the scenario, e.g. the characteristics that would be taken into account regarding Stuart.

The discussion on diminished responsibility, in comparison, is lighter. Again, it lacks citation and application to the question. The candidate therefore loses significant opportunities to achieve AO2 marks, considering his/her knowledge base.

The candidate has also failed to provide a conclusion, which is not only important for AO3 marks but is exceptionally important for AO2, as the candidate can conclude regarding the potential criminal liability of the defendant.

■ ■ ■

E-grade answer

Stuart is potentially liable for murder. However, there is a defence of provocation available to him which, if successful, would reduce his charge to manslaughter.

Murder is a common-law defence. To be found guilty of murder, Stuart must satisfy the *actus reus* and *mens rea* of murder. The *actus reus* of murder is causing death of another human being, under the Queen's peace, within any country of the realm. For the first part of the *actus reus*, Stuart has caused death of Hannah ('Stuart takes out a knife and stabs Hannah'), therefore but for Stuart's conduct, Hannah's death would not have happened. Stuart is also more than a minimal or trifling link to Hannah's death, and this makes him the legal cause of her death. Hannah is classed as a human being, as she is not a foetus or in a vegetative state, and she was killed in the Queen's peace, in a country of the realm, therefore the *actus reus* for murder has been satisfied. The *mens rea* of murder is malice aforethought. Stuart therefore satisfied the *actus reus* and *mens rea* of murder. However, there are two potential defences that Stuart can use.

Stuart is provoked by Hannah when she throws her drink at him. At this point, Stuart picks up a knife and kills her. This is a sudden and tempory [sic] loss of control, as stated in *R* v *Dutty* [sic]. This satisfies part of the elements of provocation. The next element of things done or said is also fulfilled, as Hannah insults him twice and then by throwing her drink at him she has done something to provoke Stuart.

Stuart is still suffering from heroin withdrawal symptoms, which can sometimes affect behavior [sic]. This could lead to an attempted defense [sic] of diminished responsability. The drugs were, however, taken voluntarily and willingly, so this reduces the chances of a defense [sic] of DR greatly, as his DR is caused by voluntary intoxication. It would be up to the jury to decide whether or not Stuart could foresee that by taking heroin it could in turn lead to behavioral [sic] problems. If the jury believes his level of foresight was high and he would know that by using heroin he could develop behavioral problems, then he cannot use the defense of DR. The law states that there is nothing more reckless than going out and voluntarily getting drunk or taking drugs. With Stuart pleading provocation, there is an objective test that he must satisfy. Would the reasonable man have lost self-control? If he satisfies this, then he has fulfilled all the elements to satisfy the defense [sic] of provocation.

e This answer is rather basic. The candidate should have planned the essay. This would have improved its focus. There is an awareness of the themes relating to murder, provocation and diminished responsibility throughout. However, these principles are

Section B

not discussed in a logical order. Case citation is poor and does not support the candidate's arguments. Compare the structure of this response with the C-grade answer.

There is an attempt to apply legal principles to the scenario. The application regarding murder is fuller, although not complete. The application in terms of provocation and diminished responsibility is inconsistent and confusing.

This candidate could have benefited from checking and reading his/her work. There are numerous mistakes that may have been minimised by proofreading at the end, such as poor spelling and incorrect case names, e.g. the repeated misspelling of 'defence' and 'behavioural', and writing 'R v Dutty' instead of R v Duffy.

Question 6

Heather is admitted to Scunthorpe Hospital in order to have a lump removed from her throat. On the morning of the operation, she is taken to an operating theatre where she is given an anaesthetic by Dave, a qualified anaesthetist. During the operation the tube supplying the air and anaesthetic becomes dislodged.

The surgeon, Mrs Ballard, notices that Heather is turning blue and alerts Dave, who has fallen asleep. The operation is discontinued but Heather is now in a coma, having been deprived of oxygen for several minutes.

Heather is taken to the intensive care unit. She remains on a life-support system for 3 weeks. Two qualified doctors, Meera and Rachel, decide that she is in a persistent vegetative state and will never regain consciousness. They turn off the life support and Heather dies.

Advise Dave, Meera and Rachel as to their potential criminal liability for the death of Heather.

■ ■ ■

A-grade answer

As there is a death, this scenario involves murder or manslaughter. There also needs to be a discussion on omissions and causation, as they are major issues in this question.

To be guilty of murder you must cause the death of another human being, in the Queen's peace, in a country of the realm. You must also have malice aforethought, which is to intend to cause death or GBH.

Meera and Rachel satisfy a significant number of the criteria for murder. There is a problem, however, in that Heather was on a life-support machine and in a vegetative state. Doctors are allowed to turn off life-support machines in certain circumstances, as outlined in *Bland*. In this case, the victim had been in a vegetative state due to the Hillsborough disaster. The doctors, with the consent of the parents, sought a declaration to switch off the life-support machine. The courts allowed this and the doctors were absolved of any potential liability. If the doctors have followed the criteria in *Bland*, there will be no liability. However, if they have not followed the criteria, there is strong potential for liability. Given the fact that the information just states that they have switched off the machine, there could be grounds for prosecution.

Even though Dave is not guilty of murder (there is no intent to kill), he could still be guilty of manslaughter. There are two main types of manslaughter: constructive act and gross negligence. The distinction between the two, according to *Bateman*, is an unlawful act, in that constructive manslaughter has an unlawful act. To be guilty of constructive act manslaughter, Dave must have performed an unlawful act, not an omission. As Dave has not performed an unlawful act, there is no liability through unlawful act manslaughter.

To be guilty of gross negligence manslaughter you must have a duty of care that has been breached causing death, and that breach was negligent. These criteria were laid down in *Adomako*, which is very similar to this situation. Dave, just like *Adomako*, has a duty of care by contract. As he let the breathing tube fall out, he did not complete his duty. There was a breach of duty, as Dave fell asleep and let the breathing tube dislodge. However, it is up to the jury to decide. The breach of duty must be grossly negligent. This was explained in *Bateman* as manslaughter that had gone beyond a matter of compensation, showing a distinct lack of regard for life. Given the similarities with *Adomako*, it is highly likely that Dave will be liable.

Dave could argue that he did not cause death due to the intervening act of switching off the life-support machine. This would be of little help, as this argument was tried in *Malcherek and Steel* and the courts refused to accept this.

There are therefore grounds for all parties to have liability. Dave, due to the similarities with the case of *Adomako*, has the strongest chance of a conviction and this will result in a discretionary life sentence. Concerning the liability of the two doctors, it will all depend on whether their situation fits into the *Bland* criteria.

e This answer covers all the elements required and does so in a methodical and structured manner. However, there are areas for development — the candidate could have cited more cases to support the answer, e.g. analysis of the ratio of *Adomako* and further explanation of the *Bland* criteria.

This candidate applies the legal principles to the scenario and uses the facts provided to support the legal argument. There is a good conclusion that sums up liability of the parties involved.

■ ■ ■

C-grade answer

The first issue that needs to be discussed is omission. This is because during the operation, the tube supplying air and anaesthetic to Heather became dislodged.

An omission is a failure to act. Omissions are created through both Parliament and the judiciary. There are five duty relationships in total and the one that is breached in this case is that of duty through contract. When Dave became a qualified anaesthetist he had a duty to perform his contract, and on this occasion failed to do this (he fell asleep) so it could result in criminal liability. A very similar case to this is *R* v *Adomako* because the anaesthetist failed to notice the breathing tube dislodging from the patient. He was found guilty of manslaughter. Therefore, if Dave is seen in the same light as *R* v *Adomako*, he could be found guilty of murder.

ℰ The candidate has mistakenly referred to murder instead of manslaughter here.

Dave, Meera and Rachel could all potentially be found guilty of murder, as Heather dies. This is because Dave was the reason why Heather was deprived of oxygen in the first place, and Meera and Rachel turned off the life-support machine as Heather was in a vegetative state.

The four *actus reus* aspects of murder are: causing the death, of a human being, under the Queen's peace, within any country of the realm.

The two main *actus reus* elements that are an issue in this situation are causing the death of a human being. Dave was the person who caused death, due to the fact he failed to notice the oxygen tube had been dislodged.

The two parts of causation are that the defendant must be the factual and legal cause of death with no intervening act. Factual evidence is based around the 'but for' test — but for the defendant's actions, the result would not have occurred. Therefore, this is true for Dave. The legal test has changed due to *Kimsey*. The defendant must now be more than the minimal cause of death. Dave again fulfils this.

However, due to the fact Dave did not switch off the life-support machine, it could be argued that the chain of causation was broken. But as shown in the case of *Malcherek* v *Steel*, switching off the life-support machine does not break the chain. Courts decided this in order to help doctors.

Dave does fulfil all *actus reus* elements. However, he may not pass the *mens rea* elements. This is using the *Woolin* definition, i.e. the defendant must intend to cause murder/GBH. The text on the case means that there is no evidence to prove that Dave intended to cause death or GBH. However, due to the fact that Dave had fallen asleep, his actions could be 'virtually certain' to lead to death/GBH. If so, then the jury should infer intent. It is up to the jury whether Dave can be found guilty of murder.

Meera and Rachel turn off the life-support machine because Heather is in a vegetative state and therefore this could be seen as her not being a human being any more.

ℰ There is a good discussion of some of the major elements concerning this question. What lets this answer down is the variation in terms of discussion. For example, the discussion on the liability concerning Meera and Rachel is weak and this is a significant part of the question. It is important when answering questions on cases with a number of defendants that you do not spend too much time discussing the liability of certain parties and neglect others.

The end of the answer is weak and lacks a conclusion. This could be due to time pressures. It may have been appropriate to bullet point a few concluding issues.

E-grade answer

The issue in this scenario is omission, and murder with possible defences to reduce the sentence to manslaughter as there has been the result of homicide. Whether Dave, Meera or Rachel have criminal liability for the end result of Heather's death is to be discussed.

With regard to Dave, he has a duty through contract to perform. He failed to do so and therefore endangered the life of Heather. Therefore, he has criminal liability for failing to act, as during the operation he failed to notice that the tube supplying the air and anaesthetic became dislodged, because he had fallen asleep. The exact same situation happened in the case of *R v Adomako*, and the anaesthetist was convicted of manslaughter. However, whether Dave has criminal liability is an issue for the jury to decide. Dave's failure to act severely endangers Heather's life, causing her to go into a coma, as she was deprived of oxygen which resulted in death.

Dave has potentially committed murder, as he caused Heather's death who was another human being, under the Queen's peace and within a country of the realm. However, Dave's *mens rea* is debatable, as he didn't intend Heather to die, and therefore the *mens rea* element of murder is not satisfied.

With regards to Meera and Rachel, the law clearly states that people on a life-support machine are seen as brain dead so are therefore not considered a person in being. This allows doctors to turn off life-support machines. Therefore, Meera and Rachel, who are both qualified doctors, will have no criminal liability for the death of Heather. *Malcherek* v *Steel*, which followed the criteria laid down in *Bland*, said it would be ridiculous and bizarre that the defendant would not be responsible for the result. The defendant in the scenario is Dave.

In conclusion, Meera and Rachel have no criminal liability and are therefore not guilty of any offence, whereas Dave is guilty of gross negligence manslaughter and therefore the sentence imposed is an issue for the jury to decide.

> *e* The introduction is confusing and contains inaccuracies. This is a poor start and with some planning and thought it could have been avoided. It would have been better to omit this paragraph and start with the second one.
>
> The response has two strong elements — the analysis of *Adomako* and the causation discussion. However, beyond this the comments are light and there is little detail in terms of AO1 or AO2.
>
> The conclusion, however, provides a good summary.

Question 7

George and his girlfriend Kaye are members of an activist group called Bunny, which is pledged to take direct criminal action, if necessary, as part of its campaign against animal testing. George and Kaye agree a plan to kill the prime minister, who has frequently spoken against the aims and methods of Bunny. They choose New Year's Eve as the date on which they will get the most publicity for their organisation.

However, unknown to George and Kaye, the prime minister has taken a last-minute skiing holiday and arranged for his identical twin brother to use his chauffeur-driven limousine and stay in his country house during this period.

George and Kaye lie in wait for the prime minister's car in a dark lane, pull out in front of it and force it to stop. Kaye fires a shot into the car. It misses the prime minister's brother and kills the chauffeur, Aki. Terrified, the prime minister's brother leaps out of the car. George chases after him and the prime minister's brother jumps off a bridge to escape and is immediately killed.

Consider what offences, if any, George and Kaye have committed.

■ ■ ■

A-grade answer

This question concerns the homicide of two people, Aki and the prime minister's brother. It will require consideration of murder, joint enterprise and transferred malice.

The law concerning murder requires the death of another human being under the Queen's peace within any country of the realm. Here, the deaths of two people have occurred and this satisfies the elements of the *actus reus*. However, causation may be a problem.

In order to cause death, the defendant must be the factual and legal cause with no intervening act. The factual element is the 'but for' test, as seen in *R* v *White* — 'but for' the defendant's conduct, the victim would still be alive. The legal element is the acceleration of death, as per *R* v *Adams*, and being more than minimal cause, as per *R* v *Kimsey*.

Both George and Kaye satisfy the 'but for' test. George chases the prime minister's brother, causing him to 'jump off a bridge to escape', while Kaye 'fires a shot and kills the chauffeur, Aki'. These circumstances also clearly show acceleration of death.

There is potential for an intervening act to break the chain of causation. In terms of the brother, this relates to the daftness test, whereas there is no intervening act for Aki and thus Kaye caused his death.

The daftness test involves a victim trying to escape the defendant and a result occurring because of that. Here, the prime minister's brother runs away from George. In order to constitute an intervening act, the victim's conduct must be so daft and unexpected that no reasonable person could foresee it. This is seen in the cases of *R* v *Williams and Davis* and *R* v *Marjoram*.

While it is for the jury to decide whether it is unreasonable, you would expect extreme reactions in these circumstances — the prime minister's brother fears for his life, so an attempt to escape is a natural reaction. Therefore the action would be foreseeable. In conclusion, both George and Kaye satisfy the *actus reus* of murder.

The *mens rea* of murder is malice aforethought. This means intent to kill or cause GBH. George and Kaye 'agree a plan to kill the prime minister'. This shows intent to kill. However, the two actual victims are not the intended victim, so this is oblique intent. Under the *Woollin* direction of virtual certainty, it would seem that death or serious injury was reasonably foreseeable by shooting at the car.

Under the doctrine of transferred malice, a defendant will be liable for a crime if they commit the *actus reus* and have the relevant *mens rea*, even if the victim differs from the one intended. This was established in the case of *R* v *Latimer*.

It would therefore seem that intent is transferred from the prime minister to his brother, and so both George and Kaye satisfy the *mens rea* of murder.

It is possible that the liability of the parties is different. Kaye kills Aki, but George chases the brother.

Under the principle of joint enterprise, when two parties agree a plan, and then carry it out with no departure, they are jointly liable. This can be seen in *R* v *Mohan* and *R* v *Stewart and Schofield*.

This therefore means that George and Kaye are jointly liable for both deaths. They would be found guilty of murder, which carries a mandatory life sentence. If the DPP's suggested reforms were implemented, the crime would be placed into a classification system, but due to the clear intent would still probably be 'murder 1', thus retaining the life sentence.

There is also potential for George and Kaye to be liable regarding conspiracy to murder, relating to the prime minister. They are planning to kill someone, similar to the gunpowder plot.

ℯ This is a very wide question. There are a number of legal issues that have to be discussed. This candidate correctly identifies these issues and discusses them to varying degrees. The discussion on causation and homicide are detailed, using a range of case law and explanation of legal principles. In comparison, transferred malice and conspiracy are only briefly discussed.

The candidate uses the question to support the answer throughout. This is a good technique and supports and adds depth to the AO2.

The answer could have been strengthened by adding a conclusion.

C-grade answer

These offences come under the 1957 Homicide Act. The issues are the murders of the prime minister's brother and the chauffeur, Aki. Transferred malice is also involved, as Aki and the prime minister's brother were not the intended victims, and joint enterprise, as it was not just one person who committed the offences.

For George and Kaye to be convicted of murder they need to have the *actus reus* and the *mens rea*. For the *actus reus* there are five elements: it needs to be death, of a human being, that happened under the Queen's peace, within any country of the realm and the act needs to be the cause of death. The 'within a year and a day' rule has been abolished.

Both situations satisfy all the *actus reus* elements, except when it comes to the prime minister's brother's death, because to cause death you must be the factual and legal cause with no intervening act. You must therefore satisfy the 'but for' test from *R* v *White*, which George does. The next test is that the death was accelerated, i.e. the life is cut short, which Aki's was, and if it were more than a minimal cause of death, which was also satisfied.

If there had been an intervening act, nobody would be liable for the murder of the prime minister's brother. However, with the 'daftness test' it would be found that the prime minister's brother reacted as the reasonable and sober person would have done in the situation by jumping off a bridge to stop himself from being shot. The act that the victim does has to be reasonably foreseeable, as per *Williams and Davis*. In this situation, extreme issues are expected, as a normal reasonable person would go to extreme measures to avoid being shot, so therefore the *actus reus* of murder is satisfied.

For the *mens rea* of murder, the defendant needs the intent to kill or cause grievous bodily harm. In this scenario, the *mens rea* for murder is satisfied, as Kaye and George 'plan to kill the prime minister'. Although the intent was for the prime minister, the two could still be liable through transferred malice, as the intent to kill was still there. The malice is transferable, so in this instance the *mens rea* of murder is satisfied.

What also needs to be taken into account is that the liabilities of the parties may be different, as Kaye fired the shot and George chased the driver. However, due to the principle of joint enterprise, they would both be liable for murder as they both share the common design to kill. They would only not be liable for the same offence if one of the parties went to the other and physically said they did not want a part in it any longer.

George and Kaye will both be liable for the deaths of Aki the chauffeur and the prime minister's brother. They would be convicted of murder, as they satisfy both the *mens rea* and the *actus reus* elements, and they would therefore receive life imprisonment.

e This answer has a good structure and identifies the major aspects of the question. It has a strong awareness of the law relating to murder, and it expands on the relevant aspects that need discussion, e.g. causation.

However, the candidate is not clear in his/her discussion of causation. In the third paragraph he/she mentions that the *actus reus* of murder will not be satisfied, and then in the fourth paragraph he/she states that the *actus reus* elements will be satisfied.

Overall, the answer lacks the breadth of discussion that is needed to attain a higher grade. There is identification and application on transferred malice and joint enterprise. However, further discussion is needed, not only in terms of application but also of case law.

The candidate attempts to apply the legal issues to the question, but greater emphasis is needed in this area. However, the response ends with an evaluative conclusion, which is important in order to give context to the question.

■ ■ ■

E-grade answer

George and Kaye plan to kill the prime minister, and this involves intention. This is the highest form of *mens rea*. There is no statutory definition of this and it has been left to the judiciary to decide. It is also important to appreciate that intention has set vocabulary. These terms are basic intent, specific intent and direct intent. This case involves direct intent, which is when a defendant wants an end result, e.g. I shoot you because I want you to die.

As the prime minister decided to go on a skiing holiday, his twin brother decided to take his place. The test of this is intent. This is similar to *Hyam* v *DPP*. The defendant had placed a burning newspaper through the letter box of the victim. The victim and her two children died. The defendant argued she had just intended to frighten. The court said she must have foreseen that death or GBH was a highly probable result from her conduct. This case was heavily criticised in the cases of *R* v *Mohan* and *R* v *Belfon*. It was decided that mere foresight that death or personal injury was highly probable was not same as having intention.

The shaping of intention has been a shambles, encouraging appeals and creating considerable uncertainty. Although *Woolin* gives some stability, there are still criticisms. Smith and Hogan note that only giving guidelines is not sufficient. Cases with similar facts will result in convictions or acquittals, depending on the make-up of the jury. The Law Commission has called for a definition of intent. It argues that foresight of virtual certainty should amount of intention.

The case also involves causation. This was taken when the fired shot missed the prime minister's brother and killed the chauffeur, Aki. Causation is the link between the defendant's act and the result, e.g. I hit you with a hammer and you die. This means my act has caused your death. It applies to all result crimes. The prosecution must show that the defendant was the factual cause — this is the 'but for' test. But for the defendant's conduct, the result would never have occurred. For example, a man stabs a woman. But for the man stabbing the woman, she would not have died. If you do not satisfy the 'but for' test, you are not the cause of the result.

Legal causes mean a number of tests. You must accelerate death and be more than a minimal cause of death. There are other legal issues, but these are only relevant when important. The defendant's conduct must be more than a minimal cause of death, e.g. *R v Foot*.

Actions of the victim might involve fright or flight. This involves the victim trying to escape from the defendant and, as a result, death or injury occurs because of that. For a defendant to be liable, they must fulfil the daftness test. This means the victim must do something daft. The prime minister's brother jumps off the bridge to escape.

The other issue in this is transferred malice. This is when a defendant will be liable for an offence if he has the necessary *mens rea* and commits the *actus reus*, even if the victim differs from the one intended.

In this case, George and his girlfriend both had the coincidence of *actus reus* and *mens rea* at the same time. It is general in criminal law that for a person's liability to be established it must be shown that the defendant committed the *actus reus* and possessed the *mens rea*.

The final thing the case involves is murder, and there is no statutory definition. Murder is a common-law offence. The *actus reus* of murder causes death, and this relates to causation. This has been done by George. Second is human being, problems occur because of people on a life-support machine and also concerning an unborn. The human was P.M. brother in his case. 3 is Queen's peace, this serves to excuse cases of enemy soldiers in war time. 4 within any country of the realm, all this phrase now means is the British citizens can be tried for murder when they commit in the UK or abroad.

The *mens rea* of murder is malice aforethought.

There is a lack of precise definition of death. Other countries have definition. This stops problems regarding people on life-support machines. There is lack of a precise definition of intention. The current guidelines to the jury may result in inconsistencies. Reform the whole of homicide by placing murder into a classification system similar to USA. The sentencing of murder I also very harsh, there should be different lengths of sentencing.

By looking at the case facts, I think George and Kaye would be guilty of murder. This is because they have had to kill and cause GBH.

To his/her credit, this candidate has identified the major elements of discussion regarding this question. He/she then discusses murder and its key elements but does so in a confusing manner. The response highlights poor technique, as can be seen in the discussion of mens rea at the start. It is approached like an essay question on oblique intent, going through the different tests that have been used and the problems the courts have had in this area.

Section B

By planning the answer and adopting a more selective approach regarding the legal discussion, the candidate could have secured more marks.

In terms of AO3, this response has a poor structure. The grammar in the last four paragraphs suggests that the candidate did not have enough time to complete his/her answer or to review it.